Criminal Law

by

Dr Roger Geary LLB PhD PGCE
Principal Lecturer in Criminal Law
Swansea Law School

First published in Great Britain 1994 by Cavendish Publishing Limited, The Glass House, Wharton Street, London WC1X 9PX

Telephone: 0171-278 8000   Facsimile: 0171-278 8080

British Library Cataloguing in Publication Data

Geary, Roger
Essential Criminal Law –
(Essential Law Series)
I Title II Series
344.205

ISBN 1-85941-124-X
Printed and bound in Great Britain

Foreword

This book is part of the Cavendish Essential series. The books in the series are designed to provide useful revision aids for the hard-pressed student. They are not, of course, intended to be substitutes for more detailed treatises. Other textbooks in the Cavendish portfolio must supply these gaps.

Each book in the series follows a uniform format of a checklist of the areas covered in each chapter, expanded treatment of 'Essential' issues looking at examination topics in depth, followed by 'Revision Notes' for self-assessment.

The team of authors bring a wealth of lecturing and examining experience to the task in hand. Many of us can even recall what it was like to face law examinations!

Professor Nicholas Bourne
General Editor, Essential Series
Swansea Law School

Summer 1994

Preface

The purpose of this book is to provide a revision aid for the under-graduate student of criminal law. It is intended to complement both the traditional textbook on criminal law and the Cavendish *Lecture Notes* series.

Seven key areas, which in combination form the essential content of most courses in criminal law, are considered both from a micro perspective, in terms of a more detailed discussion of the essential issues which figure prominently in examinations, and from a macro perspective, in the form of concise revision notes. A separate chapter is devoted to each of these areas containing a checklist, a consideration of relevant problematic issues, and comprehensive revision notes.

Where appropriate the most recent cases, legislation and academic articles are analysed to provide the reader with the up-to-date information necessary for success in today's competitive market-place.

I have endeavoured to state the law as at 1 July 1994.

Roger Geary
Swansea
July 1994

Table of contents

1 General principles of criminal law

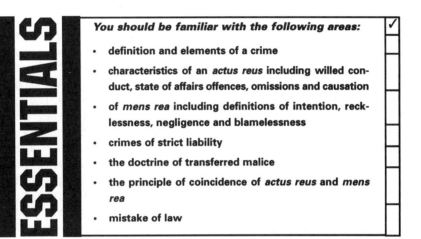

ESSENTIALS

You should be familiar with the following areas: ✓

- definition and elements of a crime
- characteristics of an *actus reus* including willed conduct, state of affairs offences, omissions and causation
- of *mens rea* including definitions of intention, recklessness, negligence and blamelessness
- crimes of strict liability
- the doctrine of transferred malice
- the principle of coincidence of *actus reus* and *mens rea*
- mistake of law

Intention

The quest for a clear concept of intention

It is somewhat surprising, given the central place which the concept of intention holds in legal theory, that not only is there no legislative definition, but also that judicial attempts to develop a definition have suffered from lack of certainty, inconsistency and disagreement. Nicola Lacey has suggested that this state of affairs is the rather unsatisfactory result of the courts attempting to establish a compromise solution between those who emphasise the importance of conceptual analysis, and those who appeal to common sense meanings ('A Clear Concept of Intention: Elusive or Illusory?' (1993) *Modern Law Review* p 621).

It can be argued that conceptual analysis is necessary in order to achieve minimum standards of formal justice. Since the criminal law can curtail the individual's freedom of action and impose heavy punishments on transgressors, it should be as clear, certain and consistent as possible. Only in these circumstances can individuals plan their lives so as to avoid coming into conflict with legal prohibitions. Not only would such conceptual clarity enable individuals to live within the law, but also it would have the benefit of rendering the criminal law more efficient from the legislator's point of view by allowing the criminalisation of only those forms of behaviour which they wish to prohibit. Moreover, conceptual analysis has the potential to contribute to substantive justice by clearly distinguishing between different degrees of culpability.

Alternatively, those who emphasise 'ordinary usage' argue that the attempt to establish precise definitions of legal concepts such as intention is both unnecessary and misguided. It is unnecessary because in everyday life terms such as 'intention' and 'dishonesty' have unarticulated, but, nevertheless, commonly understood meanings. The interpretation and application of such concepts are, therefore, best left to the 'common sense' of the jury and the lay magistrate. Indeed, it would be misguided to try to attempt a conceptual analysis of these terms since this would be likely to undermine 'ordinary' or 'common sense' meanings and shift the balance of decision making power from the lay participants in the criminal justice system to the professional lawyers. Of course, the validity of the appeal to 'ordinary language' depends on the as yet unanswered empirical question of to what extent do shared understandings inform the linguistic usage employed by criminal law.

As Nicola Lacey points out, the courts have attempted to establish an intermediate position in which the resort to 'ordinary meanings' is buttressed by recourse to conceptual analysis and stipulative definition. This approach can be seen in relation to dishonesty under the Theft Act 1968. Section 2 provides a negative definition of situations where the defendant will not be dishonest which is supplemented by the jury's 'common sense' notions of dishonesty under the Ghosh test. An analysis of the recent cases relating to intention reveals an attempt to establish a similar compromise solution.

Direct intention

The concept of direct intention appears to represent something of a fusion between conceptual analysis and widely shared everyday meanings. As Smith and Hogan note (*Criminal Law* (1992) 7th ed p 53):

Everyone agrees that a person intends to cause a result if he acts with the purpose of doing so. If D has resolved to kill P and he fires a loaded gun at him with the object of doing so, he intends to kill. It is immaterial that he is aware that he is a poor shot, that P is nearly out of range, and that his chances of success are small. It is sufficient that killing is his object or purpose, that he wants to kill, that he acts in order to kill.

However, the courts have consistently held that intention includes not only purpose, but also foresight of certainty in that a defendant can be said to have intended a result if he or she realised that the result was certain to follow from the behaviour in question. It is in relation to this second extended meaning of intention that the consensus between ordinary linguistic usage and conceptual analysis breaks down.

Indirect intention

It is convenient to say that a consequence is *directly* intended if it is the defendant's purpose or desire to produce it, and that it is *indirectly*, or obliquely, intended if it is a foreseen, but undesired consequence. Of course, common English usage would be unlikely to describe a defendant as having intended a result that he foresaw, but did not necessarily desire. Instead of reflecting common sense meanings the concept of indirect intention represents an assertion by the judges that behaviour with foresight of certainty of consequences should be classified as falling within intention rather than the lesser category of recklessness. It follows that someone who does an act in the knowledge that death or grievous bodily harm is practically certain to result should incur liability for murder rather than manslaughter. The justification for this is that the defendant's behaviour shows no respect for the value of human life; there is little moral or social difference between doing an act with the purpose of killing another and doing an act with foresight of the certainty of death.

A major difficulty with the concept of indirect intention has been the attempt to clarify what is meant by 'foresight of certainty'. Since few events in life are absolutely certain, the phrase 'foresight of certainty' is generally taken to mean practically or relatively certain. In other words it seems to be accepted that people foresee the 'certainty' of future events in terms of probability. I can foresee my own death as 100% certain, but I foresee surviving until my 70th birthday with a far lesser degree of certainty. However, once we accept the notion of relative certainty the problem arises as to what precise degree of certainty is required in order to constitute indirect intention. It is this relationship between foresight and intention which has been at the heart of a series of modern cases on the *mens rea* of murder.

From 'high probability' to 'natural consequence'

The first of the modern sequence of cases is *Hyam v DPP* (1975), in which a majority of the House of Lords were of the opinion that a person could be held to intend a result which he had foreseen as a highly probable (or perhaps merely probable – the decision is not clear on this point) consequence of his act. This is much wider than 'certainty' and consequently much further removed from common sense meanings. The problem with this definition of indirect intention was that it swallowed up a large part of what had traditionally been considered to be recklessness, while at the same time it did not provide a very clear means of distinguishing between the two concepts.

In *R v Moloney* (1985), the House of Lords departed to some extent from the analytical approach in *Hyam* by holding that judges should generally avoid attempting to define 'intention', it being preferable to leave the jury to apply their common sense understanding of the term. However, in exceptional cases, for example, where the defence argues that the defendant's purpose was only to frighten, not to harm, the victim, the judge would need to offer guidance on the meaning of intention. In these cases the jury should be directed to consider whether the defendant foresaw the prohibited consequence as 'a natural consequence' of his behaviour. If the answer to this question is 'yes' then the jury would be entitled to *infer* intention. Although Lord Bridge did provide some indication of what he meant by the phrase 'natural consequence', cases where the consequence was 'little short of overwhelming', or 'virtually certain', he, unfortunately, couched the suggested guidelines to the jury in terms of 'natural consequence'.

There are several important points to note about the decision in *Moloney*. First that foresight of a 'natural consequence' was to be considered as *evidence* of, but not the same thing as, intention. Secondly, that the decision represents an attempt to underpin common sense understandings of the term 'intention' with a more analytical approach. Finally, the phrase 'natural consequence' is inherently ambiguous in that it could be understood by the jury in several different ways.

From 'natural consequence' to 'virtual certainty'

In *R v Hancock and Shankland* (1986), two miners taking part in a strike in South Wales had been convicted of committing a murder by dropping large concrete blocks over a bridge when a taxi carrying a working miner had approached. It was argued by the defence that the miners, who had been prepared to plead guilty to manslaughter, had intended to block the road and frighten other miners into supporting the strike, but not to kill or cause serious injury. The trial judge had given the jury the *Moloney* guidelines and they inferred intent on the basis that the defendants had foreseen death or serious injury as a natural consequence of their behaviour. The Court of Appeal quashed the convictions, the Lord Chief Justice expressing considerable doubt as to the correctness of the *Moloney* guidelines which could be understood by the jury in several different ways. There then followed an appeal by the Crown to the House of Lords which was dismissed. Lord Scarman, speaking on behalf of all the Law Lords sitting on the appeal, felt that the *Moloney* guidelines on the relationship between foresight and intention were unsatisfactory in that they were likely to mislead a jury.

Lord Scarman confirmed the 'ordinary usage' approach expressed by Lord Bridge in *Moloney* to the effect that in the majority of cases juries should be left to determine for themselves whether a defendant intended a particular consequence. Where, however, a jury requested some guidance from the judge, he should explain to them that intention was not to be equated with foresight of consequences, but that it could be inferred if there was evidence of foresight. In these circumstances juries should be told that:

'The greater the probability of a consequence the more likely it is that the consequence was foreseen, and that if that consequence was foreseen the greater the probability is that that consequence was also intended.'

Clearly, this direction represents an attempt to restate the *Moloney* guidelines without reference to the ambiguous phrase 'natural consequences'. However, although ambiguity is dispensed with, uncertainty is not. Lord Scarman does not indicate precisely what degree of foresight is required to justify a jury inferring that the defendant had the necessary intent. The fundamental issue of whether a defendant intends a consequence which he foresees as possible, probable, highly probable or almost certain was addressed by the House of Lords in *R v Nedrick* (1986). Lord Lane CJ attempted to synthesise the judgments in *Moloney* and *Hancock and Shankland* by stating that:

Where the charge is murder and in the rare cases where the simple direction is not enough, the jury should be directed that they are not entitled to infer the necessary intention, unless they feel sure that death or serious bodily harm was a virtual certainty (barring some unforeseen intervention) as a result of the defendant's actions and that the defendant realised that such was the case.

This decision clarifies the position in that juries are now entitled to infer intention from foresight of *virtual certainty*.

In summary, it now appears that a defendant directly intends those consequences of his action which are his purpose (ie those consequences which he foresees and desires), quite irrespective of the probability of their occurrence. A jury may also infer that a result is intended, though not necessarily desired, when it is a virtual certain consequence of the defendant's act, and the defendant knows that it is a virtually certain consequence.

Criticisms of the existing law

Following the decision in *Hyam* a defendant could be held to have intended a result which he foresaw as highly probable (or probable), but, as we have seen, the combined effect of *Moloney, Hancock* and *Nedrick* has been to narrow the *mens rea* requirement to foresight of virtual certainty. One criticism of this development is that it imposes too high a burden on the prosecution. According to this standpoint if the accused does an act which he foresees is highly likely to cause a prohibited consequence he should be criminally liable for that consequence.

However, a major difficulty with the above argument is that such a broad conception of intention would swallow up a large part of recklessness. Moreover, the definition of intention in terms of 'high probability' lacks certainty to a greater extent than that based on 'virtual certainty'. It is not clear precisely what would count as a 'high probability' – a 60%, 70%, 80% or 90%+ chance of a consequence occurring – whereas 'virtual certainty', especially as reformulated in the Draft Criminal Code, as something that '... will occur in the ordinary course of events', leaves rather less room for doubt.

Another criticism focuses on the requirement that, as presently formulated, not only must the defendant foresee the prohibited consequence as a virtual certainty (ie a *subjective* requirement), but also it must actually be a virtual certainty (ie an *objective* requirement). Of course, the fact that a result was objectively a virtual certain consequence of the defendant's act is strong evidence that he foresaw it as such; but it is difficult to see why it should be a necessary condition of liability based on intention. After all, if a defendant mistakenly thinks that a prohibited result is a virtually certain consequence of his action surely he is just as culpable as if it were inevitable. A person who thinks he knows that the death of another will be the virtually certain consequence of his actions is just as morally blameworthy as the person who actually knows that this is the case.

The emphasis placed in both *Moloney* and *Hancock* on the exceptional nature of the cases where it is necessary for the judge to provide guidelines on the meaning of intention has been questioned. Surely the sort of cases where the defendant claims that he 'only intended to frighten' are not as rare as their Lordships suppose. Moreover, the frequency with which the juries in the above cases asked for further advice about the meaning of intention tends to indicate that the issue cannot simply be left to be resolved on the basis of a shared 'common sense' understanding of the term.

Finally, the result of the distinction which the courts have drawn between a jury inferring intention and intention itself appears illogical. If juries are entitled to *infer* intention from foresight of virtual certainty, then it follows that intention itself is something other than foresight of virtual certainty. Yet the courts have failed to indicate precisely what this something else consists of. Lord Lane CJ, in a House of Lords debate on murder, recognised the force of this criticism and suggested that the concept of intention does encompass foresight of virtual certainty, and that it is the reference to 'inferring' which is inaccurate. It seems that what the courts meant to establish is that the concept of intention includes both purpose and foresight of the virtual certainty of a particular consequence.

The confusion in the case law resulting from misplaced emphasis on 'inferring' and 'common sense' understanding seems to have arisen as Nicola Lacey, in the article mentioned above, concludes from the attempt to combine conceptual analysis with reliance on ordinary linguistic usage. She concludes that the analytical quest for an absolute valid concept of intention is illusory while the idea of a socially produced concept of intention has proved elusive. Lacey's solution is for criminal law scholars to adopt a greater commitment to socio-legal analysis. In the meantime the definition contained in Clause 18(b) of the Draft Criminal Code appears to express clearly what the House of Lords has failed to on no less than three separate occasions (ie *Moloney*, *Hancock* and *Nedrick*):

A person acts 'intentionally' with respect to ... a result when he acts either in order to bring it about or being aware that it will occur in the ordinary course of events.

Objective recklessness

Conscious and unconscious risk taking

In the landmark decisions of *MPC v Caldwell* (1982) and *R v Lawrence* (1981) the House of Lords extended the definition of recklessness to encompass the unconscious as well as the conscious taking of a risk which would have been obvious to a reasonable person. *Caldwell* was a decision concerning criminal damage while Lawrence involved what was then the offence of causing death by reckless driving contrary to s 1 of the Road Traffic Act 1971.

Both these decisions appeared to cut across the traditional distinction between different forms of liability, based on the defendant's degree of culpability. The orthodox position had developed on the assumption that liability for serious offences should be linked to a subjective *mens rea* of intention, or recklessness where the defendant *adverted* to, or foresaw, the risk. Negligence, consisting of *inadvertence*, or non-contemplation of risk, was considered less blameworthy and, therefore, not appropriate for the most serious offences, with the notable exception of involuntary manslaughter.

Interestingly, Lord Diplock, in *Caldwell* did not support the dramatic break with the traditional subjectivist approach by explicitly objectivist reasoning to the effect that a person who fails to give any thought to an obvious risk is just as socially dangerous as the person who realises the risk. On the contrary, he attacked the advertence/inadvertence distinction by arguing that subjective recklessness was unsatisfactory because it excludes the equally culpable state of indifference. Indeed, it can be argued that a person who has the capacity to appreciate a risk of harm that a reasonable person would recognise, but fails to do so, is more culpable than another person who knowingly takes a slight risk of the same harm. According to this view, inadvertence amounts to a sort of subjective negligence since the defendant chose not to consider the risk in question.

The wider application of *Caldwell* recklessness

The critique, embodied in *Caldwell*, of the traditional subjectivist position initially appeared to stand up well. After all, the orthodox emphasis on awareness of risk did, indeed, appear to narrow the ambit of recklessness too far; excluding both acts done in temper and those committed with indifference to an obvious risk. Consequently, it seemed for a while that the new objective definition of reckless was destined to be applied to offences other than those of criminal damage and reckless driving. In *Kong Cheuk Kwan* (1985) and *R v Seymour* (1983) the Privy Council and the House of Lords respectively held that objective or inadvertent recklessness should apply to manslaughter, thus, rendering killing by gross negligence virtually redundant. Moreover, *Caldwell* reckless was also held to apply to the non-fatal offences of rape (*R v Pigg* (1982)) and assault (*DPP v K* (1990)).

Criticisms of *Caldwell* recklessness

However, before long there seemed to be a growing recognition among both academic lawyers and some members of the judiciary that the *Caldwell* definition was both unduly complex and, contained the seeds of injustice.

In *R v Reid* (1992), no less eminent a judge than Lord Browne-Wilkinson admitted:

Although after long and careful analysis of Lord Diplock's direction with the help of very skilled counsel, I have, I think, understood it and find it legally correct, I cannot believe that a direction in that abstract conceptual form is very helpful to a jury.

Obviously, if a member of the House of Lords finds such difficulty in understanding the complexities of the *Caldwell* direction there can be little hope for the average juror.

Judicial disquiet with *Caldwell* recklessness does not appear to be limited to its sheer complexity, but also extends to its unethical nature. When coupled with later decisions which give an objective meaning to the phrase 'obvious risk' the effect of the *Caldwell* definition is to criminalise people who, through no fault of their own, are not capable of meeting the standard of foresight of the reasonable person. Thus, in *Elliot v C* (1983), an educationally subnormal 14 year old girl was found guilty of criminal damage for setting fire to a shed even though her appreciation of the risk involved could not match that of the reasonable person. If subjective *Cunningham* recklessness could be regarded as too narrow then objective *Caldwell* recklessness could appear too broad.

The retreat from *Caldwell*

In view of the above concerns it is not surprising that the courts have retreated to some extent from their earlier decisions. Thus, in relation to rape, the objective *Caldwell* test applied in *Pigg* was rejected in *R v Satnam and Kewal* (1983) where the requisite element of recklessness was said to exist if the accused '... could not care less whether (his victim) wanted to (have sex) or not, but pressed on regardless ...'. Similarly, in *R v Spratt* (1991) the court, overruling *DPP v K* (1990), held that *Cunningham* and not *Caldwell* recklessness should apply to assault. In *R v Savage* (1991), the House of Lords confirmed that *Cunningham* should apply to all non-fatal offences against the person that could be committed recklessly.

Moreover, the sphere of operation of *Caldwell* recklessness has been further curtailed by the replacement of the statutory offences of reckless driving, and causing death by reckless driving by dangerous driving and causing death by dangerous driving (s 1 Road Traffic Act 1988, as amended by the Road Traffic Act 1991).

Most significantly, perhaps, the Court of Appeal, in *R v Prentice and Others* (1993), decided that *Caldwell* recklessness has no general application to manslaughter. However, in order to distinguish *Seymour* it was made clear that this was a case of 'motor manslaughter' which was unaffected by the present decision. Thus, it appears that *Caldwell/Lawrence* will apply to what is in effect a new common law offence of 'motor manslaughter' which exists in addition to the statutory offence of causing death by dangerous driving. This seems to have been a neat device for escaping from the binding effect of the decision in *Seymour*, but one that is hardly satisfactory in terms of principle, not least because previously there was no separate offence of 'motor manslaughter'. Indeed, the decision on which reliance was principally based in Prentice was that of *Andrews v DPP* (1937), itself a case of killing by driving, in which Lord Atkin said:

The principle to be observed is that cases of manslaughter in driving motor cars are but instances of a general rule applicable to all charges of homicide by negligence (...) it will appear that the law of manslaughter has not changed by the introduction of the motor vehicles on the road. Death caused by their negligent driving ... is to be treated in law as death caused by any other form of negligence.

In summary, *Caldwell/Lawrence* recklessness can now only form the requisite *mens rea* for the offences of criminal damage and 'motor manslaughter'.

Caldwell modified

Given the judicial retreat, in *Savage* and *Prentice*, from imposing liability based on objective recklessness it might be thought that it would only be a question of time before *Caldwell/Lawrence* would be overruled and the concept of recklessness limited to conscious risk-taking. However, in *R v Reid* (1992), the House of Lords specifically refused to do this and strongly endorsed the ethical reasoning of Lord Diplock in both *Caldwell* and *Lawrence* to the effect that responsibility in criminal law should extend beyond those who appreciate the risks they run to those who culpably fail to do so. Nevertheless, this was not an unqualified endorsement of objective recklessness. On the contrary, their

Lordships recognised the relevance of the defendant's capacity to recognise risk to the issue of responsibility, thus, directly addressing one of the major criticisms of the *Caldwell* definition of recklessness.

This important limitation on *Caldwell/Lawrence* recklessness occurred in the following way. When counsel for the appellant realised that the attempt to get *Lawrence* overruled was failing, he sought to introduce what Lord Ackner described as a 'gloss' by arguing that *mens rea* would be lacking '... if ignorance of the relevant risk was attributable to incapacity due, for example, to the age or mental capacity of the defendant'. A majority of their Lordships appeared to accept this point. Lord Goff suggested that a defendant may drive dangerously and yet not be guilty of reckless driving where while driving he '... is affected by illness or shock which impairs his capacity to address his mind to the possibility of risk ...'. Similarly, Lord Keith accepted that Lord Diplock's model direction in *Lawrence* might have to be modified in some cases, for example, '... where the driver acted under some understandable and excusable mistake or where his capacity to appreciate risks was adversely affected by some condition not involving fault on his part'. Lord Browne-Wilkinson appeared to extend this argument from capacity to foresee the *possibility* of risk to capacity to assess the *magnitude* of risk, in his view there would be no criminal liability '... where, despite the defendant being aware of the risk and deciding to take it, he does so because of a reasonable misunderstanding, sudden disability or emergency which render it inappropriate to characterise his conduct as being reckless'.

It seems clear, then, that the majority of their Lordships were prepared to accept the need to exclude from the *Caldwell/Lawrence* definition of recklessness those who, through no fault of their own, lack the capacity to foresee the relevant risk and, possibly, those who do foresee the possibility of risk, but lack the capacity to assess its magnitude. In one sense the decision in Reid is of limited importance since the offences of driving recklessly and causing death by reckless driving have been abolished and replaced with dangerous driving and causing death by dangerous driving (s 1 Road Traffic Act 1991). However, by addressing the most powerful criticism of the concept of objective recklessness the decision has the potential to provide a sounder ethical underpinning for the development of a concept of inadvertent recklessness.

Of course, the precise scope and procedural framework of any incapacity exception still needs to be established. In their article, 'The capacity for recklessness' (*Legal Studies* (1992) p 74), Stewart Field and Mervyn Lynn suggested that the relevant incapacity should be limited to situations '... where the defendant would not have foreseen the risk, no matter how important it might be to his or her own interests to do so and therefore no matter how hard he or she tried'. Moreover, Field and Lynn argue that there should be a rebuttable presumption that defendants are capable of foreseeing those risks that the reasonable person would see as obvious. The evidential burden would initially rest on the defence to produce some evidence of incapacity, but once such evidence had been adduced the burden would shift to the prosecution to prove beyond reasonable doubt that the defendant did possess the capacity to foresee the risk, or that the incapacity relied upon was culpably self-induced.

Whether or not this kind of approach finds favour remains to be seen, but the decision in *Reid* has at least given the judiciary the opportunity to steer the law in this direction if they are so minded.

Revision Notes

The definition and elements of a crime

Definition

What sort of behaviour amounts to a 'crime' varies both historically and geographically. For example, in February 1994, the House of Commons voted to reduce the age of consent for homosexual intercourse from 21 to 18 years, whereas in many other European jurisdictions the relevant age is 16. It follows that a 19-year-old male would be committing a crime by having homosexual intercourse in the UK prior to 1994, but not after the enactment of the relevant legislation, nor in most other European jurisdictions either before or after this date. Given this relativity, any definition of 'crime' must refer not so much to the *behaviour* in question, but to the legal *status* attached to that behaviour.

A 'crime', therefore, is simply conduct which has been defined as such by statute or by the common law.

The elements of a crime

It is a general principle of the criminal law that a person may not be convicted of a crime unless he has acted in a prohibited way with a defined state of mind. The prohibited act is called the *actus reus* and the state of mind the *mens rea* of the crime.

The main exceptions to the above principle are 'state of affairs' offences, where no conduct as such need be established, and crimes of 'strict liability', where no *mens rea* need be proved (see below).

The prosecution must prove the existence of the *actus reus* and the *mens rea* beyond reasonable doubt. This is sometimes referred to as the 'Woolmington rule' (*Woolmington v DPP* (1935)).

Characteristics of an *actus reus*

Definition

An *actus reus* consists of all the elements in the statutory or common law definition of the offence except the accused's mental element.

Analysis of the *actus reus*

An *actus reus* can be identified by looking at the definition of the offence in question and subtracting the *mens rea* requirements of 'knowingly', 'intentionally', 'recklessly', 'maliciously' or 'negligently'. What is left can generally be further analysed into the central conduct of the offence, the surrounding circumstances in which it takes place and, sometimes, its consequences.

This process of identifying and analysing an *actus reus* can be illustrated in relation to s 1(1) of the Criminal Damage Act 1971 which provides:

A person who without lawful excuse destroys or damages any property belonging to another intending to destroy or damage any such property or being reckless as to whether such property would be destroyed or damaged shall be guilty of an offence.

Once expressions relating to the *mens rea* requirements of intention or recklessness have been subtracted, it becomes clear that the *actus reus* consists of destroying or damaging property belonging to another. The act which causes the destruction or damage constitutes the central conduct, the fact that the property must 'belong to another' can be regarded as the required circumstances, while the consequences consist of the resultant destruction or damage.

The conduct must be willed

Where, as is usually the case, the *actus reus* of an offence specifies some form of conduct it must be proved that the defendant consciously willed the relevant action.

If the defendant's muscles acted without the control of his mind he is not blameworthy and will be able to plead *automatism* (*Bratty v AG for Northern Ireland* (1963)).

Evidence of an 'external factor' is crucial to establish a plea of automatism (*R v Quick* (1973); *R v Sullivan* (1984)). Where the cause of the behaviour in question is 'internal' such as a 'disease of the mind' or a disease of the body the relevant defence will be that of insanity rather than automatism (*R v Hennessy* (1989)).

Impaired, reduced or partial control by the defendant will not found a defence of automatism. A total loss of voluntary control is required (*AG's Reference No 2 of 1992* (1993)).

If the defendant is at fault in bringing about the autonomic state, for example, by voluntarily taking dangerous drugs, he will have a defence to crimes of 'specific intent', but not to those of 'basic intent' (*R v Lipman* (1970); *R v Bailey* (1983)).

State of affairs offences

A crime may be so defined so as not to require any willed action at all; it may be enough if a specified 'state of affairs' is proved to exist. For example, s 4 of the Road Traffic Act 1988 provides that a person who, when in charge of a motor vehicle on a road or other public place, is unfit to drive through drink or drugs, commits an offence. It is not the action of *taking* charge of the vehicle or that of *becoming* unfit which constitutes the offence, but simply the state of *being* unfit.

Thus, the defendant in *R v Larsonneur* (1933) was convicted of being found in the UK, contrary to the Aliens Order of 1920, despite the fact that she had been forcibly brought into the jurisdiction by the immigration authorities.

Similarly, the defendant in *Winzar v Chief Constable of Kent* (1983) was convicted of being found drunk on the highway, despite the fact that he had been deposited there by police officers.

'State of affairs' offences are often also offences of 'strict liability' (see below). It is not surprising that they tend to be regarded as unjustifiably harsh, since not only is there no need to prove any action by the defendant, but also there is no need to prove any *mens rea* either.

Omissions

As a general rule, a person is not criminally liable for what they do not do. However, there are several exceptions where the defendant will be under a positive duty to act:

- duty arising from statute (eg the duty under the Road Traffic Acts to report accidents involving injury);
- duty arising from a parental or family relationship (*R v Gibbens* and *Proctor* (1918); *R v Instan* (1893));
- duty arising from contract (*R v Pittwood* (1902));
- duty to limit the harm caused by the defendant's accidental acts (*R v Miller* (1983));
- duty owed where an undertaking has been given and there is reliance on that undertaking (*R v Stone and Dobinson* (1977)).

Causation

If the definition of an offence specifies a particular consequence, then it is 'result crime' and the prosecution must prove, in order to establish the *actus reus*, that the defendant *caused* that consequence.

For example, in order to establish the *actus reus* of homicide it is necessary to prove that the defendant caused the death of the victim within a year and a day.

Causation in fact

The first step in establishing causation is to ask 'was the defendant's act a *cause in fact* of the specified consequence (eg death in the case of homicide)? This question can be answered by asking 'But for what the defendant did would the consequence have occurred?'. If the answer is no, the result would not have occurred but for what the defendant did, then causation in fact is established.

An example where the prosecution failed to establish causation in fact is the case of *R v White* (1910). The defendant had put cyanide into his mother's drink, but the medical evidence showed that she died of heart failure before the poison could take effect. Consequently, the answer to the question 'But for what he did would she have died?' is 'yes'. She would have died anyway.

Causation in law

Just because the prosecution establish that the defendant's act was a cause in fact of the consequence, does not necessarily mean that the defendant is liable. It is also necessary to prove that the defendant's act was a *cause in law* of the specified consequence.

One approach to establishing causation in law is to consider whether the defendant's act was an 'operative and substantial' cause of the consequence in question. Only if the defendant's act could be said to have merely provided the setting in which some other cause operated would the chain of causation be broken (*R v Smith* (1959)).

It should be noted that 'substantial' in this context simply means more than a very trivial cause which would be ignored under the *de minimis* principle.

Moreover, an 'operative' cause need not be the sole or main cause of the specified consequence (*R v Benge* (1865)).

An alternative approach to the 'operative and substantial' test for establishing causation in law is to consider whether the result specified in the *actus reus* was a *reasonably foreseeable* consequence of what the defendant had done. Thus, in *R v Pagett* (1983), the defendant was held to have caused the death of a girl hostage he was holding in front of him when he fired at armed police officers who returned fire, killing the girl. It was reasonably foreseeable in the circumstances that the officers would instinctively return fire and hit the victim.

The 'thin skull' rule

Even if injury or death is not a reasonably foreseeable consequence of the defendant's act, he would still in law have caused that result if the victim suffered from some physical or mental condition that made him or her especially vulnerable. This is known as the 'thin skull' rule which provides that the defendant must take his victim as he finds him. For example, in *R v Blaue* (1975) the defendant was held to have caused the death of a Jehovah's Witness who he had stabbed, notwithstanding that she had refused a blood transfusion that would have probably saved her life. He had to take his victim as he found her, including not just her physical condition, but also her religious beliefs.

Self neglect

Similarly, although it may not be reasonably foreseeable that the victim will neglect his wounds, it seems that such neglect will not break the chain of causation (*R v Smith* (1959)).

Death caused by medical treatment

Where death is caused by the medical treatment of a wound, the original attacker is held liable for homicide. This is so even in the case of *negligent* medical treatment (*R v Smith* (1959)).

However, it seems that *grossly negligent* medical treatment would break the chain of causation (*R v Jordan* (1956)).

There is some authority for the suggestion that the administration of pain saving drugs which incidentally shorten life by a very short period (hours or days, but not weeks or months) would not amount to a cause in law of death (*R v Adams* (1957)).

The nature of *mens rea*

Definition

The term *mens rea* refers to the mental element in the definition of a crime. This mental element is usually denoted by words such as 'intentionally', 'knowingly', 'maliciously', 'recklessly' or 'negligently'.

Intention

There are two types of intention; direct and indirect (or oblique). Generally, crimes which require that the defendant acts intentionally can be committed with either type.

Direct intention

Direct intention consists of foreseeing and desiring the consequence of one's conduct (ie a result is intended in this sense when achieving it is the actor's purpose).

Indirect intention

A jury may infer that a result is indirectly intended, even though it is not desired, when (1) the result is a *virtually certain* consequence of the act, and (2) the actor knows that it is a virtually certain consequence (*R v Hancock* (1986); *R v Nedrick* (1986)).

Recklessness

There are two types of recklessness known as *Cunningham* recklessness and *Caldwell* recklessness after the names of the cases which established them. Both forms of recklessness require the taking of an unjustified risk; that is, doing something which a reasonable person would not do in the same circumstances, but in some instances at least, proof that the defendant consciously took that risk is also necessary.

Cunningham recklessness

In *R v Cunningham* (1957), the defendant tore a gas meter from the wall of an unoccupied house and in so doing fractured the gas pipe, leaving gas leaking out. The escaping gas percolated into a neighbouring house and was inhaled by the occupant, endangering his life. The defendant was convicted under s 23 of the Offences Against the Person Act 1861 of maliciously administering a noxious thing so as to endanger life. However, he successfully appealed on the ground that the trial judge had misdirected the jury by telling them that 'malicious' meant simply 'wicked'. The Court of Criminal Appeal held that '... the word 'maliciously' in a statutory crime postulates foresight of consequence'. Cunningham would only have been guilty if he knew, when he broke the meter from the wall and left the gas to escape, that it might be inhaled by someone.

In order to be reckless in the *Cunningham* sense (or, indeed, malicious) it is not enough that if the defendant had stopped to think it would have been obvious to him that there was a risk; he must actually know of the existence of the risk and deliberately take it. In short *Cunningham* recklessness is the *conscious taking of an unjustified risk*.

It now seems settled that *Cunningham* is of relevance for all nonfatal offences which can be committed recklessly (*R v Savage* (1991)).

Caldwell recklessness

In *MPC v Caldwell* (1982), the House of Lords decided that where a statute uses the word 'reckless' a different type of recklessness to that defined in *Cunningham* should apply. Lord Diplock said that a person is reckless whether any property would be destroyed or damaged if:

(1) he does an act which in fact creates an obvious risk that property would be destroyed or damaged and (2) when he does the act he either has not given any thought to the possibility of there being any such risk or has recognised that there was some risk involved and has nonetheless gone on to do it.

Caldwell recklessness, therefore, consists of the *conscious or unconscious taking of an obvious risk*.

Under both limbs of the *Caldwell* direction it must be proved that the risk taken was 'obvious', but it is not clear whether the risk must be obvious to the individual defendant or to the reasonable person.

Cases such as *Elliot v C* (1983) constitute authority for an objective interpretation of the phrase 'obvious risk'. However, the House of Lords in *R v Reid* (1992) have indicated that a defendant who is not capable of appreciating a risk, which would be obvious to a reasonable person, through no fault of his own, should not be considered reckless.

It follows from the definition of *Caldwell* recklessness that a defendant will not be liable if he considered whether there was a risk and mistakenly decided that there was no risk, or a 'negligible' risk. This mental state would not constitute the conscious taking of an obvious risk, because the defendant has decided that there is no risk, nor would it amount to the unconscious taking of an obvious risk, since the defendant has considered the possibility of such a risk. The existence of this 'loophole' or 'lacuna' in *Caldwell* recklessness has now been acknowledged by the House of Lords in *R v Reid* (1992).

Two important crimes which can be committed with a *mens rea* of *Caldwell* recklessness are motor manslaughter (*R v Seymour* (1983)) and criminal damage (*MPC v Caldwell* (1982)).

Negligence

A negligent action is one that a reasonable person would not commit in the same circumstances.

Gross negligence consists of a major deviation from the standard of reasonable behaviour.

Two offences which can be committed with a *mens rea* of gross negligence are involuntary manslaughter (*R v Prentice and Others* (1993)) and causing death by dangerous driving contrary to s 1 of the Road Traffic Act 1988 as amended.

Blamelessness

A person is blameless if they have acted reasonably in the circumstances. However, even 'blameless' behaviour can attract criminal liability. Such crimes are known as crimes of 'strict liability'.

Crimes of strict liability

Definition

An offence of strict liability is one that does not require proof of fault.

Statutory interpretation

Crimes of strict liability are almost always the creation of statute. However, Parliament has rarely specified that no *mens rea* is required, preferring to leave the point to the courts to decide.

The presumption in favour of *mens rea*

Where Parliament creates a criminal offence, but fails to specify any requisite *mens rea*, the courts presume that the offence involves proof of fault, unless there is clear evidence to the contrary (*Sherras v De Rutzen* (1895)), an approach confirmed by Lord Scarman in *Gammon (Hong Kong) Ltd v A-G of Hong Kong* (1984).

However, even when a court decides that *mens rea* is required, it may not be necessary for the prosecution to prove it in relation to every element of the *actus reus*. For example, in *R v Lemon and Gay News Ltd* (1979), in relation to blasphemous libel, it was held sufficient for the prosecution to prove an intention to publish. There was no need to establish an intention to blaspheme.

The courts will regard the statute as a whole

In deciding whether or not to impose strict liability the courts will have regard to the statute as a whole. It follows that if a section creating a particular offence is silent as to *mens rea* whereas other offences under the same Act expressly require proof of fault, then the court is entitled to infer that the offence is one of strict liability (*Kirkland v Robinson* (1987)).

Regulatory offences

Where the offence is regarded as 'regulatory' or 'quasi-criminal' the courts are more prepared to impose strict liability (*Pharmaceutical Society of Great Britain v Storkwain* (1986)).

The courts are more likely to impose strict liability in these cases if they view the potential harm to society posed by the defendant's conduct to be greater than any injustice to the individual resulting from liability without fault.

On the other hand the more serious the offence the less likely the courts are to impose strict liability. In particular, they will be reluctant to impose liability without fault where there is evidence that the defendant took all reasonable care (*Sherras v De Rutzen* (1895)).

Possession of controlled drugs

Following the rather confused decision of the House of Lords in *Warner v MPC* (1970) and the subsequent enactment of the Misuse of Drugs Act 1971, it seems that the courts will impose a degree of strict liability in relation to the possession of controlled drugs.

Section 5 of the Misuse of Drugs Act 1971 creates the offence of possessing a controlled drug. To constitute this offence all the prosecution had to prove was that the defendant knew that he was in possession of a container holding 'something', and that in fact it held a controlled drug (*R v McNamara* (1988)). However, s 28(3)(b)(i) of the Act greatly limits the effect of s 5 by providing that a defendant should be acquitted if '... he proves that he neither believed nor suspected nor had reason to suspect that the substance ... in question was a controlled drug'.

In *Sweet v Parsley* (1970) the defendant was convicted of '... being concerned in the management of premises used for the smoking of cannabis', contrary to s 5(1)(b) of the Dangerous Drugs Act 1965, despite the fact that she did not know or suspect that her tenants were engaging in this practice. However, on appeal the House of Lords quashed her conviction on the grounds that since the offence was serious or 'truly criminal' proof of *mens rea* was required.

It seems that following an initial enthusiasm for imposing strict liability in relation to offences concerning possession of controlled drugs there has been both a legislative and judicial tendency to require *mens rea* for these offences.

Arguments for strict liability

Harm prevention
The main purpose of the criminal law is to prevent harmful activity. It is, therefore, illogical to confine criminal liability to those occasions where the harmful consequence is brought about with *mens rea*. The harmful consequence that the law seeks to prevent is the same whether it is intended or whether it is not.

Public protection
There are many situations where the public requires protection from negligence and the imposition of strict liability may make the potential harm-doer more careful.

Efficacy
The necessity of proving *mens rea* results in 'guilty' people escaping liability and involves the criminal justice system in additional costs and delay.

Arguments against strict liability

Strict liability is unnecessary
Strict liability results in the conviction of people who are completely blameless.

Strict liability is unjust
It is unjust that someone who has behaved impeccably could be convicted of a criminal offence and acquire a criminal record.

Negligence is sufficient
The imposition of criminal liability on the basis of negligence for regulatory offences would achieve a better balance between protecting the public and treating the individual in a just fashion.

Transferred malice

If the defendant with the *mens rea* of a particular crime, does an act which causes the *actus reus* of the same crime, he is guilty, even though the result, in some respects is an unintended one. Thus, in *R v Latimer* (1886) the defendant was found to be correctly convicted of malicious wounding, when the blow that he had stuck with his belt lightly bounced off the intended victim and injured a bystander.

However, if the defendant with the *mens rea* of a particular crime does an act which causes the *actus reus* of another crime, he will not be liable under the doctrine of transferred malice (*R v Pembliton* (1874)).

Coincidence of *actus reus* and *mens rea*

The *mens rea* must coincide at some point in time with the act which constitutes the *actus reus* (*R v Jakeman* (1983)).

Sometimes the courts have been prepared to hold that the *actus reus* consisted of a continuing act and that the defendant is liable if he formed the requisite *mens rea* at some point during this continuing act (*R v Thabo Meli* (1954); *R v Church* (1966)).

It seems that the continuing act will continue for as long as the defendant is about the business of committing or covering up the crime (*R v Le Brun* (1991)).

Ignorance or mistake of law

Ignorance of the *criminal* law is no defence, but a mistake of *civil* law maybe a defence to a criminal charge, provided it negates the *mens rea* for the offence in question (*R v Esop* (1836); *R v Smith* (1974)).

2 Incitement, conspiracy and attempt

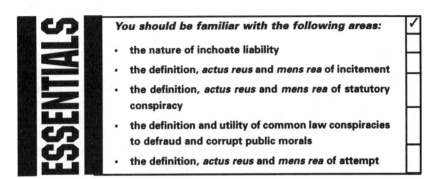
Statutory conspiracy

Intention to carry out the agreement

It would appear that the *mens rea* of conspiracy requires proof that the defendant intended to agree on the commission of a particular offence and proof of an intention that the offence should be committed. Indeed, the very essence of conspiracy, like the other inchoate offences of incitement and attempt, is the intent to cause the forbidden result. This fundamental aspect of the offence was emphasised by the Law Commission ('Report on Conspiracy and Criminal Law Reform' Law Commission No 76):

Both must intend that any consequences specified in the definition of the offence will result and both must know of the existence of any state of affairs which it is necessary for them to know in order to be aware that the course of conduct agreed upon will amount to the offence.

The draft bill introduced into Parliament also reflected the importance of an intention to cause the prohibited consequences by providing that where a person was charged with conspiracy to commit an offence:

... both he and the other person or persons with whom he agrees must intend to bring about any consequence which is an element of that offence, even where the offence in question may be committed without that consequence actually being intended by the person committing it.

Although this provision was not enacted because it was thought too complex, it was clearly conceded that the law should require full intention and knowledge before a conspiracy could be established (HL Deb vol 379, col 55).

The significance of insistence on full intention of this kind is well illustrated by the Court of Appeal's decision in *R v Siracusa* (1989). The defendants had been convicted of conspiring to import cannabis resin from Kashmir, and heroin from Thailand. Under the relevant legislation, cannabis was classified as a drug of Class B, while heroin was classified as a drug of Class A. In order to obtain a conviction for the completed offence of being knowingly concerned in the prohibited importation of controlled drugs the prosecution must prove that the defendant knew that the drugs were prohibited. However, there is no need for the prosecution to prove that the defendant knew what class of controlled drug he was dealing in.

In dismissing the defendants' appeals, the court held that the *mens rea* for conspiring to commit an offence was not necessarily to be equated with that required for the completed offence. In the present case the prosecution had to prove against each defendant that he knew that the Kashmir operation involved cannabis and that the Thailand operation involved heroin. On the facts the court was satisfied that the trial judge had made this requirement abundantly clear in his summing up.

The requirement of a full intention to bring about the consequences of the crime in question can be further illustrated by reference to the law of murder. In order to obtain a conviction for the completed offence of murder the prosecution must prove that the defendant either intended to kill or intended to cause grievous bodily harm. However, in order to obtain a conviction for conspiracy to murder it would be necessary to prove against each member of the conspiracy nothing less than an intention to kill.

The retreat from full intention

In *R v Anderson* (1986), the House of Lords appeared to retreat from the requirement that a conviction for conspiracy required nothing less than proof of a full intention to bring about the consequences of the crime in question. The defendant, who had been convicted of conspiring to effect the escape of a prisoner, appealed on the basis that he had lacked the *mens rea* necessary for conspiracy. Although he had received a payment of £2,000 as an advance payment for his part in the escape plan and had agreed to supply diamond wire that could be used to cut through prison bars, he had never intended the plan to be put into effect and believed that it could not possibly succeed.

Since it was clear that two or more of the alleged co-conspirators did intend to carry out the agreement, the defendant's conviction could have been upheld on the ground that he had aided and abetted the conspiracy. Nevertheless, their Lordships dismissed the appeal and held that all that is required to establish the *mens rea* of a statutory conspiracy is proof that the defendant intended to agree on a course of conduct which he knew would involve the commission of an offence and, as Lord Bridge, stated:

> ... beyond the mere fact of agreement, the necessary *mens rea* of the crime is, in my opinion, established if, and only if, it is shown that the accused, when he entered into the agreement, intended to play some part in the agreed course of conduct in furtherance of the criminal purpose which the agreed course of conduct was intended to achieve. Nothing less will suffice; nothing more is required.

In holding that the *mens rea* of conspiracy consists of an intention to agree and an intention to play some part in carrying out the agreement, Lord Bridge was clearly motivated by social defence policy considerations to ensure that a defendant could be convicted of conspiracy regardless of whether he desires the commission of the offence agreed on. This is an important consideration since a defendant may be indifferent as to whether the object of the conspiracy is achieved and may even hope that the other parties to the agreement are arrested before they can put their plan into operation. For example, the defendant may agree to provide a fast car for a gang to use in a robbery and yet not care whether the crime is actually committed or not. According to Lord Bridge:

> ... Parliament cannot have intended that such parties should escape conviction of conspiracy on the basis that it cannot be proved against them that they intended that the relevant offence or offences should be committed.

It appears, on policy grounds, that the House thought that it would impose too onerous a burden on the prosecution if an intention to commit the full offence had to be proved against every defendant.

Criticisms of *Anderson*

The decision of the House of Lords in *Anderson* has been subject to much critical comment. One obvious point, not withstanding Lord Bridge's comments noted above, is that the clear intention of Parliament was that nothing less than a full intention that the complete offence be committed should constitute the *mens rea* of the offence. Indeed, during the debate on the Bill in the House of Lords, the Lord Chancellor stated (HL Deb vol 379, col 55):

What has been sought to be done, and what I think has been conceded in the speeches made today, is that the law should require full intention and knowledge before conspiracy can be established.

Moreover, critics point out that the policy considerations of social defence could be achieved in situations such as the robbery example, noted above, by charging the defendant who supplies the getaway car, but who does not care whether the robbery takes place or not, with aiding and abetting rather than conspiring to commit the offence.

Perhaps the main criticism of the decision is that Lord Bridge's comments seem to indicate that a defendant could be convicted of conspiracy even if he lacked an intention that the full offence be committed, but, as Smith and Hogan (*Criminal Law* (1992) 7th ed p 273) have noted:

... if no intention needs to be proved on the part of one alleged principal offender in conspiracy, it need not be proved on the part of another. A conspiracy which no one intends to carry out is an absurdity, if not an impossibility.

Indeed, it would be very strange if intention or knowledge is required in relation to the facts or circumstances constituting an offence, but not in relation to the specified consequences.

Finally, critics have pointed out that although the decision in *Anderson* seems to have been motivated by crime control and public protection policy considerations, the effect of the judgment, at least in some situations, would be to prevent culpable defendants from being convicted. For example, if A agrees with B that B will murder A's wife, there is no conspiracy if A does not intend to play an active part in carrying out the plan.

An unintended intention?

The Court of Appeal in *R v Siracusa* (1989) attempted to overcome some of the criticisms outlined above by suggesting that it was necessary to interpret Lord Bridge's comments in the context of his judgment as a whole. It was said that Lord Bridge had not intended to suggest that a defendant could only be guilty of conspiracy if he could be shown to have intended to have played some active part in carrying out the common plan. On the contrary, Justice O'Connor noted that:

... participation in conspiracy is infinitely variable, it can be active or passive ... consent, that is the agreement or adherence to the agreement can be inferred if it is proved that he knew what was going on and intention to participate in the furtherance of the criminal purpose is also established by his failure to stop the unlawful activity.

It would appear that a conspirator can now play a part simply by agreeing that others should carry out the commission of the offence in question.

Impossibility

The issue of whether there can be liability for an inchoate offence in circumstances where the completed offence is impossible to achieve can appear confusing. However, there is one situation where it is quite clear that there is no liability for any of the inchoate offences. This is where the completed offence is 'impossible' in the sense that the intended result is not a crime at all. Thus, in *R v Taaffe* (1984) a defendant who attempted to import foreign currency into the UK in the mistaken belief that this constituted an offence could not be criminally liable. The intention he had to import foreign currency was not the *mens rea* of any offence.

The law relating to other forms of impossibility is somewhat more complex. Statutory conspiracy and attempt are governed by statute, while impossibility in relation to incitement and common law conspiracy are still subject to common law rules.

Incitement

Initially, the courts adopted a very straightforward approach to the problem of impossibility in relation to incitement. In *R v McDonough* (1962), the defendant was convicted of inciting butchers to receive stole meat carcasses notwithstanding that at the time of the incitement they may not even have existed, let alone have been stolen. On appeal it was held that the conviction should stand as the essence of the offence lay in the making of the suggestion accompanied with *mens rea*. Both these elements could be established notwithstanding the non-existence of the stolen meat.

However, during the 1970s the House of Lords took the opportunity to reassess the common law on impossibility in relation to attempt and conspiracy in the cases of *Haughton v Smith* (1975) and *DPP v Nock* (1978). These decisions ran counter to the principle in *McDonough* by holding that impossibility could, in certain circumstances, amount to a valid defence to conspiracy and attempt.

Clearly, it was illogical for impossibility to be irrelevant for the purposes of incitement while constituting a valid defence to attempt and conspiracy. The Court of Appeal attempted to resolve this inconsistency in *R v Fitzmaurice* (1983). The defendant had been asked by his father to find someone prepared to rob a woman taking wages to a bank. A man was encouraged to take part in the robbery and the defendant was subsequently convicted of incitement. He appealed on the ground that what he had incited was impossible to carry out since the planned crime was a fiction thought up by the defendant's father in the hope of obtaining reward money from the police. In dismissing the appeal the court held that the law relating to impossibility as stated in relation to conspiracy and attempt should also apply to incitement.

Moreover, it was also held that in determining the availability of a defence based on impossibility in relation to incitement, a distinction had to be drawn between 'specific' incitements and 'general' incitements. If the incitement related to a specific person or thing then impossibility, for example, the prior death of the person or the destruction of the thing, would prove a defence. On the other hand, if the incitement related to something general such as a suggestion to rob a passer-by then the offence was not really impossible since a victim could be found if the participants waited long enough.

On the basis of the decision in *Fitzmaurice*, the present position in relation to incitement would appear to be that impossibility will afford a defence to specific incitements, but not to general incitements. This is hardly a satisfactory state of affairs when, under the Criminal Attempts Act 1981, which was already in force at the time of the decision, impossibility is no longer relevant to either attempts or statutory conspiracy. It would appear that the inconsistency between the inchoate offences that the court in *Fitzmaurice* sought to rectify had been already addressed by Parliament, albeit on the basis of very different principles. In addition, there is the obvious practical difficulty of distinguishing between specific and general incitements.

In their commentary on the Draft Criminal Code, the Law Commission stated:

We believe that as far as possible there should be consistency between these (ie inchoate) offences. They share a common rationale concerned with the prevention of substantive offences and they frequently overlap.

This seems obviously right and underlines the anomalous position of the present law.

Statutory conspiracy

Section 5 of the Criminal Attempts Act 1981 which amends s 1(1) of the Criminal Law Act 1977, makes it quite clear that impossibility is no bar to conviction for statutory conspiracy. The effect of the provision is to judge defendants on the basis of the facts as they honestly believe them to be. It follows that there is a statutory conspiracy where two defendants agree to kill a person who, unknown to them, has already died. The fact of the proposed victim's death is no bar to liability, provided they honestly believed the victim to be alive and had an intention to kill.

Common law conspiracy

As we have seen, the common law offences of conspiracy to defraud and conspiracy to corrupt public morals or outrage public decency have been specifically preserved by s 5 of the Criminal Law Act 1977. Clearly, the common law rules relating to impossibility will apply to these types of conspiracy. These rules were developed, in relation to attempt in *Haughton v Smith* (1975) and for conspiracy in *DPP v Nock* (1978). The result of these decisions is that impossibility will generally be a defence to a common law conspiracy, except where the impossibility relates to the inadequacy of the proposed means of committing the offence.

Attempts

Section 1(2) and (3) of the Criminal Attempts Act 1981 provides:

(2) A person may be guilty of attempting to commit an offence to which this section applies even though the facts are such that the commission of the offence is impossible.

(3) In any case where:

(a) apart from this subsection a person's intention would not be regarded as having amounted to an intent to commit an offence; but

(b) if the facts of the case had been as he believed them to be, his intention would be so regarded, then for the purposes of subsection (1) above he shall be regarded as having an intention to commit that offence.

The plain effect of these two subsections is that for both statutory conspiracy and attempt, provided there is an immediate intention to commit the complete offence, the fact that the offence is impossible is of no relevance. All the prosecution are required to prove is an intention to commit the offence together with an agreement to commit it, in the case of conspiracy, or a more than merely preparatory step towards its commission in the case of an attempt.

However, initially the courts seemed reluctant to interpret the Criminal Attempts Act in a way which would give effect to the plain intention of Parliament. In *Anderton v Ryan* (1985), the House of Lords refused to accept that the defendant's mistaken belief that goods were stolen was sufficient to establish liability for attempted handling. However, in *R v Shivpuri* (1985) their Lordships held that s 1 of the Criminal Attempts Act 1981 was to be interpreted as requiring the defendant to be judged on the facts as he believed them to be. This decision overruled *Anderton v Ryan* and *Haughton v Smith*, in relation to attempt and statutory conspiracy, in the manner clearly intended by Parliament.

Revision Notes

Inchoate liability

Inchoate liability can occur where the defendant progresses some way towards the commission of an offence, but does not necessarily commit the completed offence.

There are three inchoate offences: incitement, conspiracy and attempt.

The prosecution have the discretion to charge a defendant with an inchoate offence even where the completed offence appears to have been committed. This strategy might be adopted where there are likely to be evidential problems with pursuing a prosecution for the full offence.

On the other hand, the prosecution are not at liberty to charge a defendant with *both* an inchoate offence and a completed crime in relation to the same criminal act.

However, where the completed offence is committed a person who has incited or conspired to commit that offence will become a participant and could incur liability as an accomplice (see Chapter 3).

Incitement

Definition

Basically, an incitement is an attempt to influence the mind of another to the commission of an offence.

Statutory incitement

There are several statutory forms of the offence, such as incitement to racial hatred and soliciting murder.

Incitement to racial hatred

Part 111 of the Public Order Act 1986 contains six offences all concerned with acts intended or likely to stir up racial hatred.

Each of the six offences require that the defendant does an act involving the use of threatening, abusive or insulting words, behaviour or material and either:

- he intends thereby to stir up racial hatred; or
- having regard to all the circumstances, racial hatred is likely to be stirred up thereby.

The offences are:

- s 18 – using threatening, abusive or insulting words or behaviour or displaying any written material which is threatening, abusive or insulting;
- s 19 – publishing or distributing written material which is threatening, abusive or insulting;
- s 20 – presenting or directing the public performance of a play which involves the use of threatening, abusive or insulting words or behaviour;
- s 21 – distributing or showing or playing a recording of visual images or sounds which are threatening, abusive or insulting;
- s 22 – providing a programme service for, or producing, or directing, a programme involving threatening, abusive or insulting visual images or sounds, or using the offending words or behaviour therein;
- s 23 – possessing written material, or a recording or visual images or sounds, which are threatening, abusive or insulting, with a view to its being displayed, published, etc.

In relation to s 18, where the defendant is not shown to have intended to stir up racial hatred, the prosecution must prove that the defendant intended his conduct to be, or was aware that it might be, 'threatening, abusive or insulting'. Where the defendant is shown to have intended to stir up racial hatred the test for establishing whether the words or conduct are 'threatening, abusive or insulting' is wholly objective.

In relation to s 22, where the defendant is not shown to have intended to stir up racial hatred, the prosecution must prove that he knew or had reason to suspect that the material was threatening, abusive or insulting. Once again, where he is shown to have an intention to stir up racial hatred, the test is objective.

For offences under ss 19, 20, 21 and 23, there is no need for the prosecution to prove an intention or awareness in relation to 'threatening, abusive or insulting', but a defendant who is not shown to have intended to stir up racial hatred may be able to raise certain defences:

- in relation to s 19, it is a defence for the defendant to show that he was not aware of the content of the material and did not suspect or have reason to suspect that it was threatening, abusive or insulting;

- in relation to s 20, it is a defence for the defendant to show that he did not know and had no reason to suspect that offending words or behaviour were threatening, abusive or insulting;
- in relation to s 21, it is a defence for the defendant to show that he was not aware of the content of the recording and did not suspect and had no reason to suspect that it was threatening, abusive or insulting;
- in relation to s 23, it is a defence for the defendant to show that he was not aware of the content of the written material or recording and did not suspect, and had no reason to suspect, that it was threatening, abusive or insulting.

Soliciting murder

Section 4 of the Offences Against the Person Act 1861 (as amended by the Criminal Law Act 1977) provides that it is an offence to '... solicit, encourage, persuade or endeavour to persuade or ... propose to any person, to murder any other person'.

This provision seems to add nothing of substance to the principles relating to incitement at common law (see below). It seems probable that the creation of a special statutory form of the offence was considered necessary in order to reflect the seriousness of the crime incited.

Incitement at common law

Definition

An incitement consists of encouraging or pressurising another to commit an offence.

Actus reus

The central conduct of the offence can take various forms such as suggesting, proposing, requesting, encouraging, persuading, threatening or pressurising another to commit an offence (*Race Relations Board v Applin* (1973)).

It is necessary that the incitement is communicated to the incitee (*R v Banks* (1873)), but there is no need for the incitee to act on the incitement (*R v Higgins* (1801)).

If the incitor tries, but fails, to communicate the incitement, then he would be liable for the offence of attempted incitement (*R v Ransford* (1874)).

The act incited must be one which the incitor believes would be a crime by the person incited. The defendant must, therefore, know or believe that the incitee has, or intend that he shall have, the *mens rea* for the offence suggested etc (*R v Curr* (1968)).

A member of a class of people that a particular offence is designed to protect cannot be liable for inciting that offence (*R v Tyrrell* (1894)). Thus, a girl under the age of 16 could not be guilty of inciting a man to have sexual intercourse with her since she is a victim that the offence of unlawful sexual intercourse is designed to protect.

Mens rea

The defendant must intend to incite and intend that the incitee act on the incitement (*Invicta Plastics v Clare* (1976)).

In addition the defendant must know of all the circumstances of the act incited which are elements of the crime in question and intend the consequences specified in the *actus reus*.

Since the *mens rea* of the person incited is included among the elements of the crime the incitor must know or believe that the incitee has the requisite *mens rea* for the offence in question (*R v Curr* (1968)).

It follows that if the defendant believes that the incitee will do the suggested act without the *mens rea* for the crime in question, then he is not guilty of incitement (even if unknown to him the incitee does have the necessary *mens rea*). In these circumstances the defendant may be liable for the completed crime, either as an abettor or as a principal offender via the doctrine of innocent agency.

Incitement and other inchoate offences

As we have noted, there is an offence of attempted incitement (*R v Ransford* (1874)), but it seems that there is no offence of inciting an attempt (Schedule 1, paras 34 and 35 of the Magistrates' Courts Act 1980).

The old common law offence of incitement to conspire was abolished by s 5(7) of the Criminal Law Act 1977, but there may be a conspiracy to incite.

At common law the offence of inciting incitement exists (*R v Sirat* (1986)). However, as we have seen, s 5(7) of the Criminal Law Act 1977 abolished the offence of inciting conspiracy. It follows that the common law offence of inciting an incitement will now only exist where the incitement is based on threats or pressure which do not amount to an incitement to conspire (*R v Evans* (1986)).

Incitement and participation

Section 30(4) of the Criminal Law Act 1977 appears to have been drafted on the assumption that there is no such offence as incitement to counsel or abet an offence.

Conspiracy

Statutory conspiracy

Definition

The statutory offence of conspiracy is created by s 1(1) of the Criminal Law Act 1977, as amended by s 5 of the Criminal Attempts Act 1981, which provides:

... if a person agrees with any other person or persons that a course of conduct shall be pursued which, if the agreement is carried out in accordance with their intentions, either:

(a) will necessarily amount to or involve the commission of any offence or offences by one or more of the parties to the agreement; or

(b) would do so but for the existence of facts which render the commission of the offence or any of the offences impossible;

he is guilty of conspiracy to commit the offence or offences in question.'

Actus reus

The *actus reus* of a statutory conspiracy consists of an agreement on a 'course of conduct' that will 'necessarily' involve the commission of an offence.

It appears that merely talking about the possibility of committing an offence is not sufficient to constitute an agreement (*R v O'Brien* (1974)).

Section 1(1), paragraph (b) of the Criminal Law Act makes it clear that, as far as *statutory* conspiracy is concerned, the fact that the agreement is impossible to carry out is no bar to liability (impossibility may still be a defence to a charge of common law conspiracy).

The agreement must be communicated between the parties to the conspiracy (*R v Scott* (1979)).

Victims, the spouse of the accused and children under 10 years of age cannot be parties to a conspiracy.

If the words '... necessarily amount to ... the commission of any offence ...' were construed strictly, it would be impossible to secure any convictions for conspiracies to commit possible offences. For example, suppose that Boris agrees with his mistress Belinda to put a deadly poison into his wife's food. At first sight this appears to be a clear case of conspiracy to murder, but it could be argued that this course of conduct would not *necessarily* have amounted to the offence in question; the wife might not be hungry or she might drop the plate, or she might not have died. Paradoxically, if the offence was impossible, perhaps because the wife was already dead at the time of the agreement, then there would be liability for conspiracy to murder since, as we have seen, impossibility is no defence.

In order to avoid this kind of anomalous result the courts have been prepared to interpret the phrase 'course of conduct' in a way which includes not just the conspirators intended actions, but also the intended consequences of those actions (*R v Reed* (1982)). According to this interpretation Boris and Belinda would be guilty of conspiracy to murder since the intended result of their common plan was the death of the wife.

Mens rea

The defendant must intend to agree on the commission of a particular offence and intend that the offence should be committed.

In addition the defendant must know or believe the circumstances specified in the definition of the offence to exist and must *intend* that the prohibited consequences occur.

Intention is required even where the offence agreed upon is capable of being committed with a lesser degree of *mens rea* (*R v Siracusa* (1989)). For example, murder can be committed with an intention to kill or cause grievous bodily harm, but to be guilty of a conspiracy to murder nothing less than an intention to kill is required.

It is sometimes suggested that Lord Bridge in *R v Anderson* (1986) held that it is not necessary to prove that the defendant intended the offence to be committed, merely that there was an intention to play some part in the carrying out of the agreement. However, the courts have tended to reinterpret, or clarify, Lord Bridge's comments in a way that makes it clear that there is no need for the prosecution to prove an intention to play a part in the common plan (*R v Siracusa* (1989); *R v Edwards* (1991)). It would now appear that a conspirator can play a part simply by agreeing that others should carry out the offence.

Common law conspiracy

Section 5(2) and (3) of the Criminal Law Act 1977 preserve two forms of common law conspiracy: conspiracy to defraud and conspiracy to corrupt public morals or outrage public decency.

Conspiracy to defraud

Many fraudulent activities will constitute substantive criminal offences and an agreement to engage in them could be charged as a statutory conspiracy. However, some fraudulent activities may not amount to a substantive offence. An agreement to engage in this kind of activity can not be charged as a statutory conspiracy, but may well result in a conviction for common law conspiracy to defraud.

An example would be where two or more people agree to *temporarily* deprive another of his property. Since there is no intention to permanently deprive the victim of property this would not amount to an agreement to steal contrary to s 1 of the Theft Act 1968, but would constitute a conspiracy to defraud.

It is not clear precisely what type of behaviour is required to amount to defrauding. In *Scott v MPC* (1975), Lord Diplock suggested that where the intended victim was a private individual the purpose of the conspirators must be to cause economic loss by interfering with some proprietary right. In the case of a public official the conspiracy to defraud should be intended to cause him to act contrary to his duty.

However, in *Wai Yu-Tsang v R* (1991), the Privy Council cast doubt on the distinction between private individuals and public officials and further held that conspiracies to defraud are not limited to cases of intention to cause economic loss. It seems that all that is required is proof that the conspirators '... dishonestly agreed to bring about a state of affairs which they realise will or may deceive the victim ...'.

The *mens rea* for conspiracy to defraud requires proof of an intention to defraud and evidence of dishonesty. In *Wai Yu-Tsang v R* (1991), Lord Goff said that intent to defraud simply meant '... an intention to practise a fraud on another, or an intention to act to the prejudice of another man's right'.

It is suggested that where dishonesty is in issue the *Ghosh* test can be applied (see Chapter 5).

Conspiracy to corrupt public morals

This common law offence is preserved by s 5(3) of the Criminal Law Act 1977 because, following the decision of the House of Lords in *Shaw v DPP* (1962), there was some uncertainty as to whether or not there was a substantive offence of corrupting public morals. Although the better view, perhaps, is that there is not.

If there is, indeed, a substantive offence of corrupting public morals then an agreement to do this would amount as a statutory conspiracy and there would be no need for the common law offence. However, it can be argued that if there is no such substantive offence then the common law offence is necessary to impose liability on those who agree to bring this consequence about.

Conspiracy to outrage public decency

It is now well established that there is a substantive offence of outraging public decency (*Knuller v DPP* (1973); *R v Rowley* (1991); *R v Gibson and Another* (1991)). The retention of the common law offence of conspiring to outrage public decency is no longer necessary as this would now amount to a statutory conspiracy.

Common law or statutory conspiracy?

According to s 12 of the Criminal Justice Act 1987 statutory conspiracy and common law conspiracy are not mutually exclusive. The prosecutor can choose which offence to charge in cases of overlap.

Impossibility

Impossibility is no defence to a charge of statutory conspiracy (s 1(1)(b) Criminal Law Act 1977), but may be a defence to a common law conspiracy (*DPP v Nock* (1978)).

In order to constitute a defence to common law conspiracy the impossibility must relate to something other than the means used to bring the offence about (*Haughton v Smith* (1975)).

Attempt

Definition

By s 1(1) of the Criminal Attempts Act 1981:

> If with intent to commit an offence to which this section applies, a person does an act which is more than merely preparatory to the commission of the offence, he is guilty of attempting to commit the offence.

Actus reus

It must be proved that the defendant has gone beyond mere preparation although it is not necessary for the 'last act' prior to the commission of the offence to have been committed (*R v Gullefer* (1987)).

Lord Lane, in *Gullefer*, said that the 1981 Act sought to steer a 'midway course' between mere preparation, on the one hand, and the 'last act' necessary to commit the offence, on the other. He went on to state that an attempt begins 'when the defendant embarks on the crime proper'.

It seems that the courts take a relatively restricted view of what amounts to going beyond mere preparation. For example, in

R v Campbell (1991) the defendant, who was armed with an imitation fire arm, was arrested within a yard of the door of a post office which he intended to rob. Nevertheless, the Court of Appeal held that there was no evidence on which a jury could 'properly and safely' find that the defendant's acts were more than merely preparatory.

The judge decides whether there is sufficient evidence to put to the jury, but it is the jury who must decide whether the defendant's acts have gone beyond mere preparation and thus come within the s 1(1) definition of an attempt (*R v Griffin* (1993)).

Mens rea

The defendant must have the intention to commit the offence in question (*Mohan v R* (1976)). Following the decision in *R v Walker and Hayles* (1990) it appears that indirect intent will suffice.

Where an offence requires *mens rea* as to a circumstance, such as recklessness as to whether the victim of rape consents to intercourse, then the prosecution will have to prove intention as to the central conduct (ie intercourse) and recklessness (of the *Cunningham* type) as to consent (*R v Khan* (1990)).

Impossibility

It is now clear that impossibility, whether factual or legal, will be no defence to a charge of attempt (*R v Shivpuri* (1986)).

Offences that can be attempted

Generally, any offence triable in England and Wales as an indictable offence (ie any offence triable only on indictment, or triable either way) may be attempted (s 1(4) Criminal Attempts Act).

However, the following offences cannot be attempted:

- statutory or common law conspiracy;
- offences of assisting an arrestable offender or compounding an arrestable offence contrary to s 4(1) and s 5(1) of the Criminal Law Act 1967;
- aiding, abetting, counselling or procuring the commission of an offence (s 1(4)(b) Criminal Attempts Act 1981).

Where aiding etc, is the principal offence as in s 2(1) of the Suicide Act 1961, an attempt to aid is an offence because this would not amount to aiding an *offence* within the terms of s 1(4)(b) of the Criminal Attempts Act 1981.

3 Participation

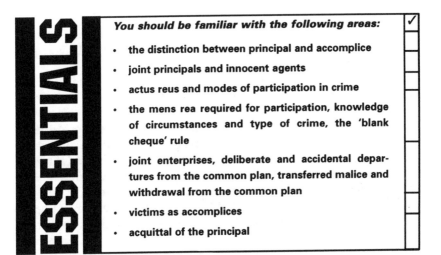

ESSENTIALS

You should be familiar with the following areas: ✓

- the distinction between principal and accomplice
- joint principals and innocent agents
- actus reus and modes of participation in crime
- the mens rea required for participation, knowledge of circumstances and type of crime, the 'blank cheque' rule
- joint enterprises, deliberate and accidental departures from the common plan, transferred malice and withdrawal from the common plan
- victims as accomplices
- acquittal of the principal

The mental element in complicity

Knowledge or purpose?

In order to satisfy the *mens rea* requirements for liability as an accomplice the defendant must intend that his acts will aid, abet, procure or counsel the principal; mere recklessness would seem insufficient. In addition, the accomplice must have knowledge of all the circumstances which constitute the *actus reus* of the offence and know that the principal intends to commit a crime of the 'type' actually committed (*Johnson v Youden* (1950); *R v Bainbridge* (1959)). These requirements apply even where the principal can incur liability for the completed offence with a lesser degree of mental responsibility such as recklessness, negligence or strict liability.

The reason for this seemingly high fault requirement, as with inchoate offences, is that the further the basis of criminal liability from the actual infliction of harm the narrower the grounds of liability should be. It is the presence of a restrictive fault requirement which controls what Glanville Williams referred to in his *Textbook of Criminal Law* as the tendency of the law of complicity to '... expand beyond reasonable bounds' ((1983) 2nd ed p 341). This tendency is particularly prevalent in relation to aiding where, for example, a bus driver who transports a murderer to his victim's address satisfies the *actus reus* requirements as does a fellow passenger who informs him that he has arrived at the correct stop. Obviously, there must be a mental element to limit liability in such situations, but there is some dispute as to precisely how restrictive this should be.

In *NCB v Gamble* (1959), a weighbridge operator issued a ticket allowing a lorry driver to take an overloaded vehicle out of the colliery onto the public highway. The Divisional Court held that the weighbridge operator was liable for aiding and abetting the driver's offence so long as he knew that the lorry was overloaded and that it was about to be driven on a public road. It was irrelevant that the weighbridge operator was 'only doing his job' and may have been indifferent as to whether the driver committed an offence by taking the lorry onto the highway. This broad approach holds that it is the defendant's knowledge of what the principal is about to do which constitutes a sufficient degree of fault.

However, there is also authority for a narrower conception of fault. In *Gillick v West Norfolk and Wisbech Health Authority* (1986), the House of Lords held that a doctor who supplies contraceptives to a girl under the age of 16, knowing that this would assist her boyfriend to commit the offence of unlawful sexual intercourse, is not an accomplice to the boyfriend's offence. The doctor was exercising his clinical judgment with the intention of protecting the girl, not with the intention of aiding the offence. At first glance this seems to confuse intention with motive. However, if 'intention' is taken to mean *purpose* type intention, where the defendant is required to foresee and desire the consequences of his actions, the decision makes sense, albeit in a very restrictive way. Clearly, this conflicts with the approach in *Gamble* where it was held that mere knowledge of assistance is enough and that purpose is not required.

Glanville Williams has suggested an intermediate position between the broad and narrow approaches in that the *Gamble* requirement of knowledge should be applied in cases of aiding and abetting, whereas the *Gillick* concept of purpose is more appropriate in cases of counselling and procuring ('Complicity, Purpose and the Draft Code' (1990) *Criminal Law Review* p 4). Another possible solution which is sometimes advocated is to support the broad knowledge based approach to *mens rea*, but to balance this by a more ready acceptance of appropriate defences. For example, the defendant doctor in *Gillick* could have been acquitted on the basis of a defence of medical necessity rather than lack of *mens rea*. Similarly, in *R v Clarke* (1985), it was held that a person who knowingly assists others to commit a burglary, with the intent that the police capture the burglars, does satisfy the *mens rea* requirements of secondary liability, but may have a defence based on his intention of assisting law enforcement.

The conflict between the broad approach adopted in *NCB v Gamble* where mere knowledge of assistance is enough and the narrow approach of *Gillick* where purpose type intention appears to be required is underpinned by precedents in favour of each view (see, for example, G R Sullivan 'Intent, Purpose and Complicity' (1988) *Criminal Law Review* p 641 and the reply by Dennis (1988) Criminal Law Review p 649). The fundamental point at issue is whether such a wide-ranging *actus reus*, consisting of aiding, abetting, counselling or procuring, requires in the interests of justice a narrow fault requirement in order to limit liability. Which position is taken in relation to this question will depend on whether *individualistic* values, favouring maximum freedom of action for the individual and minimum responsibility for the actions of others, or *collectivist* values, emphasising social responsibility, are adopted. It is at this point that law inevitably links with politics.

The rule in *Bainbridge*

In the above discussion we noted a conflict between the dominant approach which holds that mere knowledge of assistance is required to establish liability as an accomplice and a dissenting approach which advocates that nothing less than purpose type intention will suffice. However, the question remains as to what precisely must that knowledge (or intention) relate to. An answer is provided by the decision of the Court of Appeal in *R v Bainbridge* (1959). The defendant had supplied cutting equipment which was subsequently used to break into a bank. He claimed that he had thought that the equipment might be used for some illegal purpose, such as breaking up stolen property, but that he had not known that it was going to be used in a bank robbery. In dismissing the appeal the Court of Appeal held that the prosecution was not required to prove that the defendant knew exactly what crime was going to be committed by the principal. Lord Justice Parker CJ stated:

... there must be not merely suspicion but knowledge that a crime of the type in question was intended, and that the equipment was bought with that in view.

It follows that the defendant must have contemplated the type of crime that may be committed by the principal when carrying out his acts of assistance. This is more restrictive than requiring a general criminal intent, in the sense of knowledge that the principal was going to commit some crime, but at the same time broader than a require-ment of detailed knowledge of the offence eventually committed. Although the rule in *Bainbridge* is couched in terms of knowledge it appears that what is actually required here is subjective recklessness. The defendant must have foreseen the risk of the principal committing a certain type of offence and yet gone on to provide assistance.

The application of the rule in *Bainbridge* to murder

Few would argue that a defendant who willingly provides assistance, knowing that one of a category of similar offences may be committed, should escape liability. However, the fact that liability for participation in English law is closely linked to the precise offence committed by the principal can cause injustice. Nowhere has this been made more clear than in relation to the offence of murder.

The *mens rea* for murder is an intention to kill or cause grievous bod-ily harm (*R v Hancock and Shankland* (1986)). However, in *Chan Wing Siu v R* (1985), the Privy Council held that it was sufficient for the pros-ecution to prove foresight of death or grievous bodily harm as a pos-sible consequence of the 'common design' or plan, being carried out in order to secure the conviction of an accomplice to murder. Such fore-sight of the possibility of death or grievous bodily harm could be inferred by the jury from the evidence of what the defendant did and said. However, the case also decides that a defendant would not be liable where the risk of death or grievous bodily harm is '... too remote to be seriously contemplated ...'. In this type of situation the jury must decide whether the risk which the accused recognised was sufficient to make him a party to the crime.

The decision can be criticised for producing an unjust result in that it appears that conscious risk-taking (ie recklessness), consisting of foresight of death or grievous bodily harm as a *possible* consequence of the common plan, can result in the accomplice being convicted of mur-der, whereas the principal can only be convicted if he foresees death or grievous bodily harm as a virtual *certainty* (*R v Nedrick* (1986)).

Moreover, an accomplice will be subject to the mandatory life sentence following a murder conviction within the UK and possibly the death sentence following appeals to the Privy Council.

This last point is illustrated by the case of *Hui Chi-Ming v R* (1992). The defendant was convicted as an accomplice to murder and was sentenced to death in Hong Kong. He had been one of a group of men who had gone out 'looking for someone to hit' after the principal's girlfriend had complained of being bullied. The principal offender hit the victim with a length of pipe causing fatal injuries and was tried for murder, ultimately being convicted of manslaughter. The defendant refused to plead guilty to manslaughter and was convicted of murder. The Judicial Committee of the Privy Council dismissed his appeal. Lord Lowry stated that all that had to be proved against the secondary party was that he had foreseen that the principal might commit such an act as part of the joint venture and had participated in it with that foresight.

In England and Wales the Court of Appeal has consistently confirmed the decision in *Chan Wing Siu* in a string of cases such as *R v Jubb and Rigby* (1984), *R v Ward* (1987) and *R v Hyde* (1990). More recently in *R v Roberts* (1993) the Court of Appeal confirmed the general approach of Lord Lane CJ in *Hyde* to the effect that:

There are, broadly speaking, two main types of joint enterprise cases where death results to the victim. The first is where the primary object of the participants is to do some kind of physical injury to the victim. The second is where the primary object is not to cause physical injury to any victim but, for example, to commit burglary. The latter type of case may pose more complicated questions than the former, but the principle in each is the same. A must be proved to have intended to kill or do serious bodily harm at the time he killed (...) B, to be guilty, must be proved to have lent himself to a criminal enterprise involving the infliction of serious harm or death, or to have had an express or tacit understanding with A that such harm or death should, if necessary, be inflicted.

Roberts also confirms *Hyde* in that there is no need for a judge to emphasise that the accomplice's foresight of death or grievous bodily harm should be of a 'real' or 'substantial' or 'serious' possibility. However, it was accepted that an accomplice who had only '... fleetingly thought of the risk of his co-accused using violence ... only to dismiss it from his mind' would not be consciously taking a risk that the principal might kill or cause serious injury. It seems that all that is required is that the prosecution prove beyond reasonable doubt, that the defendant realised that the principal offender might kill or intentionally cause serious injury, and that he, nevertheless, continued to participate in the joint venture. This is the case even where weapons were not carried, and where the object of the unlawful enterprise was burglary or robbery, and not physical injury.

In *R v Rook* (1993), the above principle was applied to a defendant who was not even present at the scene of the crime. The accused and three other men planned to kill the wife of one of them in return for a payment of £20,000. Although the defendant took an active part in planning the murder, he did not intend that it should actually take place. He believed, wrongly as it turned out, that if he did not turn up as planned the others would not go ahead without him. He was convicted and appealed on the grounds that there had been misdirections about the *mens rea* necessary to establish liability as an accomplice and as to what amounts to an effective withdrawal. In upholding the conviction, the Court of Appeal held that it was no defence for an accomplice to say that he did not intend the victim to be killed if he contemplated or foresaw the killing as a real or serious risk. Moreover, the mere fact that the defendant absented himself on the day of the murder did not amount to an unequivocal communication of his withdrawal from the agreement to murder, and therefore he could not escape liability.

Although it may be logical that an accomplice who was not present at the scene of the crime should be in the same position as if he had been present, the question remains, should *either* be convicted of murder? Why should an accomplice who foresees death or grievous bodily harm as a *possible* consequence of the joint venture be guilty of murder, whereas the principal, who after all is the one who actually kills, must be shown to have foreseen death or grievous bodily harm as a *virtual certainty*?

Professor JC Smith has attempted to explain the present position by recognising that the accomplice's liability is based on recklessness and then distinguishing recklessness as to whether death results (which is sufficient for manslaughter, but not for murder) from recklessness as to whether a murder be committed. In other words, the accomplice's liability is based on recklessness not directly as to the death, but indirectly in relation to the principal's intention to kill or cause grievous bodily harm. The liability of the accomplice, thus, *derives* from that of the principal. While this explanation may be theoretically satisfying it hardly addresses the serious concerns raised by cases such as *Hui Chi-Ming*. A suggested solution would be to create a separate crime of facilitation, to be committed by anyone who assists a person who is known to be involved in a crime (see RJ Buxton 'Complicity in the Criminal Code' (1969) *Law Quarterly Review* p 252). This would have the advantage of allowing the facilitator to be sentenced according to the level of seriousness of the crime contemplated.

Unfortunately, the opportunity for reform seems somewhat muted as Clause 27(1) of the Draft Criminal Code merely restates the existing law, albeit in more modern language. It is, therefore, difficult to disagree with the conclusion of Nicola Padfield ('The High Risk of Participation in Criminal Activities' (1993) *Cambridge Law Journal* p 373) that:

... Clause 27, accepting as it does the risk-based theory of liability, should not be adopted wholeheartedly. Recent cases add strength to the argument that complicity liability should be confined to cases where it is the accomplice's intention (or even, perhaps, his purpose) that the perpetrator should commit the crime. But if a risk-based test is acceptable, then fairness demands that it should be a test of high probability, not just possibility. Whatever the test the mandatory life sentence is inappropriate.

In short, foresight of the possibility of death or grievous bodily harm is so far removed from foresight of the virtual certainty of death or grievous bodily harm that the existing law offends the generally accepted principle of fairness that like cases should be treated alike.

A possible exception?

The rule in *Lomas's* case

It seems that a defendant may escape liability as an accomplice even though he has aided the principal by supplying him with the means of committing an offence and has knowledge of the offence which the principal intends to commit. This exception to the general rules relating to secondary liability occurs where the accomplice would incur some liability under the civil or criminal law by not providing the act of assistance or encouragement. For example, in *R v Lomas* (1913), the defendant returned a crowbar to its owner, knowing that it would be used to commit burglaries. It was held that the defendant had not incurred liability as an accomplice since had he deliberately retained the crowbar he could have been liable for the tort of conversion and, possibly, theft.

The case of *Gillick*, discussed above, could also be interpreted in a way which provides support for this principle. It will be remembered that the doctor was found not guilty of aiding unlawful sexual intercourse by prescribing contraceptives to a girl under the age of 16 because he was exercising his clinical judgment. This could be taken to mean that merely carrying out the obligations of employment could not amount to aiding in the same way as performing other contractual obligations could not.

Similarly, in *R v Salford Health Authority ex p Janaway* (1988), a doctor's secretary was dismissed for refusing to type a letter referring a patient to a hospital for an abortion. She sought a judicial review of her dismissal by the Area Health Authority on the ground that, as a Roman Catholic, she did not want to aid the carrying out of an abortion. The Court of Appeal, ultimately held, that she could not be described as aiding, counselling or procuring an abortion by merely carrying out an obligation under her contract of employment.

Criticism of the rule

The above principle can be criticised in that it attaches greater importance to civil property rights and obligations than it does to the prohibitions of the criminal law. This approach clearly contrasts with the generally accepted view that it is the criminal law which is concerned with more serious obligations which extend '... beyond a mere matter of compensation between subjects ...' *(per* Hewart LCJ in *R v Bateman* (1925)).

According to this view the law should not exempt from secondary liability those who in performing contractual obligations knowingly assist the principal offender to commit a serious crime. For example, suppose a gunsmith contracts to sell a shot-gun to X and before delivery discovers that X intends to murder his wife with the gun. According to the principle as stated in *Lomas* the gunsmith would not incur liability as an accomplice by delivering the gun in accordance with his contractual obligations, but both ethics and a policy of crime prevention suggest that he should.

Another criticism is that the rule is unnecessary in that if the defendant honestly believed that he was under a legal obligation to engage in the acts of assistance, then he would lack the mental element for secondary liability under ordinary principles of *mens rea*. Of course, this point is only valid if a purpose as opposed to a knowledge based concept of *mens rea* is adopted.

The Draft Criminal Code

Under Clause 27(6)(c) of the Draft Criminal Code Bill a defendant would be exempted from liability as an accomplice where he aided the commission of an offence while under the belief that he was legally obliged to do so and did not have as his purpose the furthering of the commission of the offence.

Preventing crime and limiting harm

Informers and undercover agents

Police officers, their informants and private citizens sometimes do acts which actually assist in the commission of an offence, albeit with the secret purpose of frustrating its commission, or getting evidence against the offenders. The common law has evolved on an *ad hoc* basis to provide limited protection rather than a blanket immunity to those who engage in this sort of activity.

Generally, the law distinguishes between those who *instigate* the commission of an offence and those who participate in an offence which is going to be committed in any event, notwithstanding that in both situations the undercover agent/informant acts in order to trap the offenders. It seems that those who instigate the commission of an offence which would not otherwise be committed can incur liability for incitement or as an accomplice (*R v Sang* (1975)). Indeed, the Law Commission has recommended not only that there should be no defence of entrapment, but also that consideration should be given to the creation of a new *offence* of entrapment ('Report on Defences of General Application' Law Com No 83, 1977; see also, Ashworth 'Entrapment' (1978) *Criminal Law Review* p 137). On the other hand, it appears to be lawful to participate in an offence which is going to be committed anyway provided the defendant does so in order to trap the offenders (*R v McCann* (1971)). These principles would seem to apply to private citizens in the same way as they apply to law enforcement agents (*R v Clarke* (1984)).

However, Smith and Hogan in their textbook *Criminal Law* ((1992) 7th ed p 158) note that the courts have in practice tended to interpret the above principles in a way which '... may have shown undue tolerance to incitement of offences by the police'. They go on to argue that:

... it cannot be the law that the police may properly participate in a crime to the point at which irreparable damage is done. A policeman who assists E to commit murder in order to entrap him must be guilty of murder. It is submitted that the same must be true of any injury to the person ... and probably to any damage to property, unless the owner consents.

If this suggestion is correct it would appear that a person who participates in a crime which was going to take place in any event, with the purpose of preventing the commission of that offence, does not himself commit an offence. However, the person who participates with the purpose of entrapment may still incur liability if the harm caused by the commission of the offence outweighs the good done by securing evidence against the offenders.

Limiting harmful consequences of crime

A rather different situation to that of the undercover agent is where an act of assistance is done with the purpose of limiting the harmful consequences of the offence in question. Of course, the provision of contraceptives to a girl under the age of 16, as in *Gillick*, would fall into this category. Other examples would include the supply of condoms to prisoners, or of sterile hypodermic needles to drug addicts, for the purpose of limiting the risk that the prisoners or addicts would become infected by the AIDS virus as a result of the anticipated criminal acts of buggery or injection.

It obviously seems wrong that defendants who do such acts of assistance, with the intention of limiting the harmful consequences of crime, should run the risk of incurring liability as accomplices. As we have seen, sometimes the courts have avoided convicting this kind of defendant by interpreting the requisite *mens rea* as consisting of 'intention' in the sense of 'purpose'. Thus, in *Gillick*, Lord Scarman referred to circumstances in which the:

... *bona fide* exercise by a doctor of his clinical judgment must be a complete negation of the guilty mind which is an essential ingredient of the criminal offence of aiding and abetting the commission of unlawful sexual intercourse.

Alternatively, as was suggested above, conviction could be avoided, at least in some of these situations, by recourse to the principle, illustrated by *Lomas's* case, that a defendant cannot assist the commission of an offence by performing a legal obligation.

Although the courts seem reluctant to do so, the injustice of convicting someone who is acting in good faith to prevent or limit the harmful consequences of the commission of an offence which is going to take place in any event could also be avoided by explicitly recognising the defence of necessity.

The Draft Criminal Code Bill

Clause 27(6)(a) provides that a person is not guilty of an offence as an accomplice by reason of anything he does with the purpose of preventing the commission of the offence. This provision probably merely restates the existing law. Clearly, those who do acts of assistance, not with the purpose of *preventing* the commission of the offence, but in order to entrap the offenders may still incur liability.

However, Clause 27(6)(b) also exempts the person who acts with the purpose of avoiding or limiting any harmful consequences of the offence and without the purpose of furthering its commission. As the Law Commission's commentary on the Draft Criminal Code makes it clear this provision could provide a defence for the police agent/informant:

Subsection (6)(a) provides for the case of the police informer or undercover agent who does acts that in fact assist the commission of an offence but whose purpose is to frustrate its commission. If his plan fails and the offence is committed before the police can intervene he is not guilty as an accessory. Subsection (6)(b) similarly protects one whose act is designed to avoid or limit the harmful consequences of an offence – for example, by enabling the police to intervene after a theft or similar offence to recover the stolen property and arrest the participants. He is not guilty as an accessory if he acted without the purpose of forwarding the commission of the offence.

Obviously, subsection (6)(b) would also protect those, like the doctor in *Gillick*, who provide assistance in order to limit the harmful consequences of an offence which is likely to committed in any event. The Law Commission noted that:

The generalisation that such acts do not attract criminal liability seems plainly right although, perhaps unsurprisingly, authority for it is lacking.

Clause 27(6)(b), therefore, provides a useful clarification of the law in this respect.

Revision Notes

The principal and the accomplice

The principal

The principal is the person whose act is the most immediate cause of the *actus reus* of the crime in question.

In murder the principal is the person who, with *mens rea*, fires the fatal shot. In theft, it is the person who dishonestly appropriates property belonging to another with an intention to permanently deprive the other of it.

The accomplice

An accomplice is someone who has helped or encouraged the principal offender to commit the crime.

Joint principals and innocent agents

Joint principals

In some cases it may be impossible to distinguish between principals and accomplices, for example, where two or more defendants stab the victim intending to murder him and the combined effect of the wounds does kill him. In these circumstances the defendants would be charged as joint principals.

The test for distinguishing between a joint principal and an accomplice would seem to be to ask whether the defendant by his own actions, as distinct from anything done by the other parties to the crime, contributed to the causation of the *actus reus*? If the answer is 'yes', then the defendant is a joint principal rather than an accomplice.

Innocent agency

If the *actus reus* of the crime in question has been brought about by the action of someone who has no *mens rea*, or who has a defence such as automatism, insanity or infancy, then that person can be termed an *innocent* agent.

In these circumstances the principal is the person whose act is the most immediate cause of the innocent agent's act. For example, if A hypnotises B and commands him to perform the *actus reus* of an offence while he is in an hypnotic trance, it is A who is the principal offender.

Modes of participation

Definition

Section 8 of the Accessories and Abettors Act 1861, as amended, provides:

Whosoever shall aid, abet, counsel, or procure the commission of any misdemeanour whether the same be a misdemeanour at common law or by virtue of any act passed or to be passed, shall be liable to be tried, indicted and punished as a principal offender.

Actus reus

The *actus reus* for secondary liability can take the form of one or more of the following modes of participation.

Aiding

Many different actions could amount to aiding. For example, driving the principal to the scene of the crime, keeping a look-out while he commits the offence or providing him with a weapon, equipment or information. All these activities have in common the fact that they help, assist or support the principal in carrying out the crime in question.

Although 'aiding' requires actual assistance in the sense that it must allow the defendant to commit the crime more easily, earlier or with greater safety, it need not *cause* the commission of the offence.

Similarly, there is no need for any agreement, or *consensus*, between the principal and the accomplice.

Abetting

This mode of participation consists of encouraging the principal to commit the offence. Usually, to amount to abetting the encouragement must be given at the time the offence is committed.

It seems that the abetting must be operative in the sense that a defendant will be liable as an accomplice only in relation to offences which are committed to some extent in *consequence* of the abetting. This is not to say that the encouragement must be a cause of the commission of the offence, but rather that there must be some connection between the abetting and the commission of the offence. There is no need for the prosecution to prove that the principal was influenced by the encouragement, but he must, at least, have been aware of it and acted within the scope of the advice (*R v Calhaem* (1985)). Abetting, therefore, implies a *degree* of consensus.

Counselling

Counselling is very similar to abetting in that it can consist of advising, encouraging, persuading, instructing, pressurising, or even threatening the principal into the commission of the offence. However, there is a difference between the two concepts in that abetting usually occurs during the commission of the offence whereas counselling takes place at an earlier stage.

Like abetting counselling implies a degree of consensus, although there is no need for the prosecution to prove causation. All that seems to be required is proof that the principal was aware of the encouragement etc and acted within its scope (*R v Calhaem* (1985)).

Procuring

Lord Widgery CJ, in *AG's Reference No 1 of 1975* (1975) stated that to procure was to 'produce by endeavour'. It seems, then, that 'procuring' simply means 'causing'.

There is no need for the prosecution to produce any evidence of consensus between the principal and the accomplice.

Mere presence at the crime

Mere presence at the scene of the crime will not be sufficient to amount to any of the above modes of participation.

In *R v Coney* (1882), it was held to be a misdirection to tell a jury that mere presence at an illegal prize fight was sufficient to amount to abetting the offence.

Similarly, in *R v Clarkson* (1971), the conviction of two soldiers who had been present in a room while other soldiers had raped a woman was quashed. The court held that the jury should have been told that they could only be convicted if (a) their presence had actually encouraged the commission of the offence, and (b) they had intended their presence to have that effect.

Obviously, abetting or counselling will occur where a spectator applauds or purchases a ticket for an illegal performance (*Wilcox v Jeffery* (1951)).

Mens rea

Intention to aid, abet, counsel or procure

The defendant must intend to do the acts which he knew were capable of assisting, encouraging or causing the commission of the crime. Thus, in *Lynch v DPP for Northern Ireland* (1975), the intentional driving of a car amounted to aiding and abetting even though the defendant was horrified by the principal's plan to shoot a policeman at the journey's end.

Knowledge as to circumstances

In addition to intending the central conduct of aiding etc, the defendant must *know* of any circumstances specified in the *actus reus* of the offence in question. This applies even to offences of strict liability (*Johnson v Youden* (1950)).

Knowledge as to the type of crime

The accomplice must have contemplated the type of crime committed by the principal when carrying out the act of assistance or encouragement, but there is no need for him to know the precise details of the offence (*R v Bainbridge* (1959)).

An accomplice can, therefore, be convicted with a far lesser degree of *mens rea* than that required to establish the guilt of the principal.

Nowhere is this principle more apparent than in relation to law of murder. The *mens rea* for murder is an intention to kill or an intention to cause grievous bodily harm (*R v Hancock and Shankland* (1986); *R v Nedrick* (1986)). However, the *mens rea* which has to be established in relation to accomplices to murder is foresight of death or grievous bodily harm as a *possible* consequence of the common plan being carried out (*Chan Wing Siu v R* (1985); *R v Hyde* (1991); *R v Roberts* (1993)).

The effect of the above principle is that a defendant can be convicted as an accomplice to murder even in circumstances where the principal lacks the *mens rea* for this offence. All that is required is that the defendant *realises* (there is no need for an agreement) that the principal *may* kill or inflict grievous bodily harm and continues to participate in the common plan. Moreover, there is no need for a judge to emphasise that the defendant's foresight of death or grievous bodily harm should be a 'real', 'substantial' or 'serious' possibility (*R v Roberts* (1993)).

The 'blank cheque' rule

Where the defendant has given the principal assistance or encouragement to commit one of a range of offences, in short, a 'blank cheque', then the accomplice will be liable for any offence that the principal actually commits within that range of contemplated offences.

For example, in *Maxwell v DPP for Northern Ireland* (1979) the defendant drove terrorists to a remote public house, knowing that they intended to commit a crime of violence, but was unsure what precise offence they intended to commit. The House of Lords held that a person could be convicted as an accomplice without proof of knowledge of the actual offence provided he contemplated the commission of one of a limited number of crimes by the principal and intentionally assisted or encouraged such a crime.

Joint enterprises

There are two situations in which liability as an accomplice can arise:

- where the defendant supports the principal by providing assistance or encouragement for his actions; and
- where the parties embark upon a joint unlawful enterprise. Such a joint enterprise will involve an attempt to implement a common plan.

Acts within the scope of the common plan

If, as a result of carrying out a common plan, the defendant contributes towards the causation of the *actus reus* of an offence he would incur liability as a joint principal.

Similarly, the defendant will incur liability as an accomplice if the principal commits any offence within the scope of those contemplated.

Accidental departure from the common plan

The general rule is that an accomplice will be liable for all accidental, or unforeseen consequences that flow from the common plan being carried out.

For example, in *R v Baldessare* (1930) the two defendants took a car to go 'joyriding' and drove off without turning on the headlights. In the dark they accidentally ran over and killed another road user. The driver was convicted of manslaughter and the passenger, Baldessare, was convicted as an accomplice to manslaughter. The killing was an accidental departure from a common plan which involved driving a car in a reckless manner.

Deliberate departure from the common plan

Where the principal deliberately departs from the common plan the other parties will not be liable in respect of any consequences of his action.

This rule was confirmed in *Davies v DPP* (1954), where the defendant was acquitted of being an accomplice to either murder or manslaughter because he was unaware that the principal intended using a knife during a fight with members of an opposing gang. Lord Simonds LC said:

... I can see no reason why, if half a dozen boys fight another crowd and one of them produces a knife and stabs one of the opponents to death all the rest of his group should be treated as accomplices in the use of a knife and the infliction of mortal injury by that means, unless there is evidence that there is intended or concerted or at least contemplated an attack with a knife by one of their number, as opposed to a common assault.

If the victim had died as a result of being punched or kicked, the defendant would have been liable as an accomplice to murder as this would then constitute an accidental departure from the common plan (*R v Betts and Ridley* (1930)).

Transferred malice

As we have seen, under the doctrine of transferred malice, if A, intending to wound, aims a blow at B, but misses and hits C, he will be liable for wounding C. The *mens rea* A had in relation to B is transferred to C (*R v Latimer* (1886)). This rule can be usefully summarised: if D brings about the *actus reus* of an offence with the *mens rea* of the same offence he is liable even though the results of his conduct are, in a sense, unintended.

However, the operation of the doctrine of transferred malice in relation to accomplices may be modified by the above rules relating to accidental and deliberate departure from the common plan.

This point is well illustrated by reference to the facts of *R v Leahy* (1985), where the defendant, Leahy, counselled the principal, Horsman, to 'glass' a man called Pearson. Horsman then picked up a glass and pushed it into the neck of a man called Gallagher. Horsman was convicted of grievous bodily harm contrary to s 18 of the Offences Against the Person Act 1861. It would not make any difference as to his liability whether he was aware or unaware that his victim was not Pearson. In the former case he would be liable under straightforward principles of *mens rea* or, in the latter, under the doctrine of transferred malice.

However, there would be a difference as far as the liability of Leahy was concerned. If Horsman was aware that his victim was not Pearson, then his attack would constitute a deliberate departure from the common plan and would, thus, relieve Leahy of any liability as an accomplice. Alternatively, if Horsman was unaware that he victim was not Pearson, then this would constitute an accidental departure from the common plan which would render Leahy liable as an accomplice to the grievous bodily harm.

Withdrawal from the common plan

Where a party has assisted or encouraged another to commit an offence certain offences, such as incitement, conspiracy and, possibly, attempt may have been committed even *before* the common plan is completely carried out (see Chapter 2). However, liability as an accomplice contrary to s 8 of the Accessories and Abettors Act 1861 only occurs *after* the contemplated offence has actually been committed. The question, therefore, arises as to under what circumstances is it possible for a party who has assisted or encouraged the offence to withdraw from the common plan prior to its completion and, thus, avoid liability as an accomplice.

What will amount to an effective withdrawal will depend upon which mode of participation the accomplice has engaged in. If the defendant has assisted or encouraged the commission of the offence prior to its commission, then it seems that all that is required is that the defendant clearly communicates his withdrawal from the common plan.

For example, in *R v Grundy* (1977) the defendant had provided information of use to burglars, but then, two weeks before the planned offence, he had tried to dissuade them from committing the crime. It was held that he was entitled to have his defence of withdrawal left to the jury.

Alternatively, in *R v Rook* (1993) the defendant and three others planned the murder of the wife of one of them. The day that the others carried out the planned murder, the defendant, without having informed the others of his withdrawal, simply failed to turn up. On appeal against conviction as an accomplice to murder, he argued that he had not intended the murder to occur and that he had effectively withdrawn by not turning up. His appeal was dismissed on two grounds:

- where in a case of joint enterprise resulting in unlawful killing the accused is charged as a secondary party, it is not necessary for the defendant to have intended death or grievous bodily harm, all that is required is that he provided encouragement or assistance intending to provide that encouragement or assistance and with foresight that death or grievous bodily harm was a possible consequence of the carrying out of the common plan;
- someone who is a party to a joint enterprise to commit an offence and who changes his mind about participating, cannot escape liability by withdrawing unless he has at least unequivocally communicated his withdrawal to the other participants.

Of course, the most unequivocal evidence of effective withdrawal would be to inform either the police or the potential victims of the planned crime. However, the law does not require the defendant to go to these lengths, leaving it for the jury to decide on a case by case basis, whether there is sufficient evidence to indicate that the defendant did enough to make it clear that he was no longer giving assistance or encouragement to the principal offenders.

Where the defendant aids or abets at the scene of the crime, then much more will be required in order to constitute an effective withdrawal. Indeed, in these circumstances nothing less than physical intervention may be required. In *R v Becerra and Cooper* (1975) the defendants agreed to burgle a house, and Becerra gave Cooper a knife to use in case there was any 'trouble'. When they were disturbed by the householder Becerra ran off shouting 'lets go'. Cooper remained behind and murdered the householder with the knife. Becerra unsuccessfully appealed against conviction as an accomplice to murder on the grounds that he had withdrawn from the common plan. It was suggested that the defendant would have to show that he had taken reasonable steps to prevent the commission of further offences in order to establish an effective withdrawal. Something 'vastly different' and more effective than simply shouting 'lets go' was required.

Victims as accomplices

In *R v Tyrrell* (1894), a girl below the age of 16 was found not guilty of aiding and abetting a man to have unlawful sexual intercourse with her. The principle was that a defendant cannot incur liability as an accomplice if the offence in question is one that was designed to protect a class of people of which the defendant is a member.

The above principle has been affirmed both by the courts (*R v Whitehouse* (1977)) and by Clause 27(7) of the Draft Criminal Code Bill.

Acquittal of the principal

No *actus reus* committed by the principal

If the principal is acquitted because he has not committed the *actus reus* of the offence in question, then the defendant will not be liable as an accomplice as there is no offence to assist or encourage (*Thornton v Mitchell* (1940)).

However, even if the principal has not committed the *actus reus* he may be liable for an attempt (see Chapter 2 above). In these circumstances the defendant could be liable for aiding and abetting the attempt.

Principal has a defence not available to the accomplice

If the principal is acquitted because he can avail himself of some defence which is not available to the defendant, there is nothing to prevent the conviction of the defendant as an accomplice.

For example, in *R v Bourne* (1952), the defendant was convicted of aiding and abetting the offence of buggery, having forced his wife to have sex with an Alsation dog. The fact that the wife was acquitted as the principal offender on the basis of duress did not effect the liability of the accomplice.

No *mens rea* on the part of the principal

If the principal is acquitted because he lacks the *mens rea* for the crime in question the defendant may still incur liability either as a principal who has acted through an innocent agent (*R v Michael* (1840)) or as an accomplice (*R v Cogan and Leak* (1975)).

4 Offences against the person

Non-fatal offences

Assault and battery

It is now settled by s 39 of the Criminal Justice Act 1988 that assault and battery are two separate offences (*DPP v Little* (1991)). However, it remains to be seen how seriously the courts will be prepared to take this distinction in relation to the interchangeability of the *mens rea* of the two offences. According to the usual principles of liability a defendant who does acts which constitute the *actus reus* of one crime with the *mens rea* of another crime is not guilty of either (*R v Pembliton* (1874)). Given that they are separate offences, there is no reason why this principle should not equally apply to assault and battery. For example, if A waves his fist with the intention of frightening B, but not with the intention of striking him and without foreseeing the possibility of making bodily contact with him, actually strikes him, A will have caused the *actus reus* of battery with the *mens rea* of assault. This disjunction between *actus reus* and *mens rea* could also occur in the opposite fashion where A is reckless as to whether he causes an impact on B, but foreseeing no possibility of causing apprehension, perhaps because B is asleep or blind, actually does cause fear. In theory A should not be liable for either assault or battery in either situation because there is no coincidence of *actus reus* and *mens rea*.

However, in the case of closely related offences the courts have sometimes held the *mens rea* of the two offences to be interchangeable. An example of this is s 170(2) of the Customs and Excise Management Act 1979, as construed by the House of Lords in *R v Shivpuri* (1985). Since assault and battery are particularly closely associated, indeed, 'inextricably confused' in some of the leading cases, it is quite possible that the courts will adopt the position of regarding the *mens rea* of the two offences as interchangeable (Smith and Hogan *Criminal Law* (1992) 7th ed p 404).

It is suggested that such an approach would be both wrong in principle and unnecessary. The appropriate charge in situations such as those cited above would be that of attempted assault in the former case and attempted battery in the latter.

Sections 47 and 20 of the Offences Against the Person Act 1861

Although in *R v Savage* (1991) the House of Lords clarified several disputed points, they have been criticised for doing so without attempting to introduce some consistency of principle into the law relating to non-fatal offences against the person. The judgment relates to two cases which were joined on appeal to the House of Lords.

In *Savage*, the defendant had intended to throw the contents of a glass of beer over another woman, but as she did so the glass broke and injured the victim. At first instance the defendant was found guilty of an offence contrary to s 20 of the Offences Against the Person Act 1861. However, the Court of Appeal found that there had been a misdirection and substituted a verdict of guilty of assault occasioning actual bodily harm contrary to s 47 of the Act. The trial judge had neglected to direct the jury that they had to find that the defendant had foreseen some physical harm, other than wetting the victim with the beer, as a result of her act.

In *Parmenter*, the defendant had caused injuries to his baby son, but argued that he had not realised that the way he handled the child would cause injury. The Court of Appeal quashed his convictions under s 20 of the Offences Against the Person Act 1861 on the ground that although the trial judge had correctly based his direction on *R v Mowatt* (1968) he had inadvertently created a risk that the jury would believe that they were being asked to consider not whether the defendant actually foresaw that his acts would cause injury, but whether he ought to have foreseen it. Moreover, the court refused to substitute verdicts under s 47 of the Act on the basis that the intent required in ss 47 and 20 was inconsistent.

In dismissing the appeal in *Savage* and upholding that in *Parmenter* Lord Ackner, in the House of Lords, in a judgment with which the other judges concurred, decided four issues raised by the two appeals:

- if an accused is charged under s 20, it is possible to convict that person under s 47 instead;
- in relation to s 47 the only mental element that needs to be proven relates to the initial assault (ie there is no need for the *mens rea* to extend to the resulting actual bodily harm);
- the word 'maliciously' in the 1861 Act embodied recklessness in the subjective *Cunningham* sense of the conscious taking of an unjustified risk;
- for s 20 it is sufficient if the accused foresaw the risk of some physical harm (ie there is no need for the defendant to have foreseen the risk of either wounding or grievous bodily harm).

Certainty without principle?

In relation to the first issue considered by the House of Lords in *Savage*, it is difficult to see how the conclusion arrived at can be justified in terms of principle. This is because the House expressly affirmed their previous decision in *R v Wilson* (1984) that an unlawful wounding or infliction of grievous bodily harm contrary to s 20 does not necessarily involve proof of an assault. Yet s 6(3) of the Criminal Law Act 1967 only allows the substitution of an alternative verdict where the offence charged amounts to or includes, expressly or by implication, an allegation of another offence. Surely for an alternative verdict under s 6(3) the offence to be substituted must *necessarily* be implied in the offence with which the accused is charged.

Once again, in relation to the second issue, there seems to have been no consideration of matters of policy and principle. As a matter of strict statutory interpretation the position stated by Lord Ackner appears to be correct and confirms the decision in *R v Roberts* (1972). Briefly this is that, in the context of s 47 the word 'assault' incorporates the *mens rea* for common assault, but since the word 'occasioning' only suggests issues of causation, there is no need for the *mens rea* to extend to the resulting actual bodily harm. However, this approach makes no attempt to try to achieve a consistent and principled approach to issues of culpability within the context of an antique piece of legislation.

Similarly, Lord Ackner's finding that *Caldwell* recklessness does not apply to offences requiring malice is certainly correct. Indeed, Lord Diplock, in *Caldwell*, made clear that his new objective concept of recklessness did not apply to 'malicious' offences such as those under consideration in *Savage*. However, no policy reasons were given as to why objective recklessness is inapplicable to offences against the person. Moreover, the House of Lords missed the opportunity to address the misgivings about the operation and applicability of *Caldwell* recklessness generally (see Chapter 1).

It is, perhaps, the confirmation of the decision in *Mowatt* that for the purposes of s 20 the defendant must have foreseen some physical harm, but not necessarily serious harm or wounding, which has been most criticised. If a statutory definition states that it is an offence, intentionally or recklessly, to cause a specific result, then principle requires that the recklessness should extend to the whole of that consequence not merely a lesser part of it. Anything less than this correspondence between *mens rea* and *actus reus* creates an offence of constructive liability.

Not only did Lord Ackner fail to give detailed consideration to the arguments of principle against this approach, but also he repeated the misleading words '.;hould have foreseen ... some physical harm' which Lord Diplock used to frame the direction in *Mowatt*. The word 'should' is ambiguous as it could be taken to imply an objective test into s 20, or it could be understood in a subjective sense as meaning that the defendant 'must have' foreseen some physical harm. In no less than four reported cases, including *Parmenter*, convictions have been quashed because an ambiguous direction on the necessary *mens rea* for s 20 was given to the jury. It is regrettable that the House of Lords did not take the opportunity to avoid further confusion by laying down a new model direction. The question is not whether the defendant should have foreseen the risk of some physical harm, but whether he did foresee such a risk. Juries could be told that the fact that a defendant should have foreseen may be evidence that he did foresee, but it is no more than that.

In short, it seems that *Savage* clarifies several important issues, but does so on the basis of inadequate reasoning and analysis. As Graham Virgo has observed 'If the House of Lords will not consider fundamental issues of policy and principle, who will?' ('Offences Against the Person – The Wheel is come Full Circle' (1992) *Cambridge Law Journal* p 6).

Battered women and provocation

The social context

One indicator of the widespread nature of domestic violence against women is that 41% of all female victims of recorded homicides in England and Wales in 1991 were killed by their partners. In contrast, only 8% of male homicide victims were killed by their partners ('Criminal Statistics 1991, England and Wales' 1993 HMSO 75). Although accurate empirical data on the topic is difficult to collect, it is not unreasonable to assume that the vast majority of the women who kill their partners would have been subjected to severe physical and emotional abuse. In recent years the increasing recognition of the existence of this sort of abuse and of the difficulties experienced by women who attempt to escape it, has focused attention upon the legal position of battered women who kill their partners. In particular, it is often argued that the law on provocation and self defence is so firmly based on male standards of behaviour as to cause considerable injustice to women in this unenviable position.

R v Ahluwalia

The operation of the law of provocation in the context of the battered woman who kills is well illustrated by the decision of the Court of Appeal in *R v Ahluwalia* (1992). The defendant's husband had began beating her only days after their arranged marriage. The violence continued over a 10-year period and included the infliction of injuries such as bruising, broken bones and teeth, scalding and being knocked unconscious. In addition, there was frequent sexual abuse and death threats. From January 1989 the violence intensified and in March the husband, who was having an affair, left home for a few days. On his return the beatings continued. Matters came to a head one evening in May. The husband demanded money for a telephone bill and threatened to beat her the next morning if it was not forthcoming. Later, he put a hot clothes iron against her face and threatened to burn her. The defendant, who had bought some caustic soda and a can of petrol with a view to using them on her husband, waited until he was asleep and then poured the petrol over him, igniting it with a candle. He received burns from which he died some days later. There was evidence that the defendant was found standing in the burning house with a glazed expression, saying 'I'm waiting for my husband.' Later she said that she had given him a fire bath to wash away his sins.

At her trial for murder the defence argued that there had been no intention to kill, merely to cause pain and, in the alternative, manslaughter due to provocation. She was convicted and appealed on three grounds:

- that the judge had misdirected the jury on provocation in that since the enactment of s 3 of the Homicide Act 1957 there was no need for there to be a 'sudden and temporary' loss of self-control;
- that the judge had also misdirected the jury by failing to attribute the characteristic of being a battered woman to the hypothetical reasonable person; and
- that the conviction was unsafe because of evidence of diminished responsibility which had not been put forward at the trial.

On the latter ground alone, the Court of Appeal set aside the conviction and ordered a retrial. At the second trial a plea of manslaughter was accepted and the defendant was sentenced to 40 months imprisonment, exactly the period already served.

Implications of *Ahluwalia* for subjective provocation

One of the reasons why the law of provocation may treat the victim of domestic violence unfairly is that the woman in this predicament is unlikely to react with instant violence in the same way that a man would. Given inequalities of physical strength such a reaction would only be likely to result in the woman suffering yet more violence. It is, therefore, perhaps, unsurprising that the research indicates that instead, of a sudden eruption of anger, battered women typically undergo a cumulative 'slow burn' of fear, despair and anger which can lead them to kill their tormentor, perhaps while he is asleep, drunk or otherwise vulnerable (see Dobash and Dobash 'The Nature and Antecedents of Violent Events' (1984) *British Journal of Criminology* p 269).

It follows that Devlin J's classic definition of provocation, laid down in *R v Duffy* (1949), as a 'sudden and temporary loss of self-control' is likely to exclude many battered women who kill. In addition the courts have tended to treat the existence of 'cooling time', any gap between the last provoking act and the killing, as precluding the defence of provocation (*R v Hayward* (1833); *R v Duffy* (1949) and *R v Ibrams and Gregory* (1981)).

In *Ahluwalia* the Court of Appeal rejected the defence contention that following the enactment of s 3 of the Homicide Act 1957 there was no longer any need to direct the jury as to the suddenness requirement. Lord Taylor CJ said that he was bound by the previous decisions and that the *Duffy* definition was so well established that it would require nothing short of legislation to change it. However, he did give some ground in relation to the 'slow burn' reaction of battered women:

We accept that the subjective element in the defence of provocation would not as a matter of law be negated simply because of the delayed reaction in such cases, provided that there was at the time of the killing a 'sudden and temporary loss of self-control' caused by the alleged provocation. However, the longer the delay and the stronger the evidence of deliberation on the part of the defendant, the more likely it will be that the prosecution will negative provocation.

This is an important passage which has the potential to open up the defence of provocation for battered women, at least to some extent. It now seems accepted that there is still the possibility of a sudden loss of self-control even after acts of preparation have been done and after the passage of time. Preparation and time delay are relegated from legally precluding the provocation defence to simply evidence as to whether self-control was actually lost. Battered women who kill their sleeping or indisposed partners following a 'slow burn' of anger are now entitled to have provocation put to the jury.

The implications of *Ahluwalia* for objective provocation

At first instance the trial judge had directed the jury to consider how a reasonable, educated, Asian woman would have responded to the provocation. On appeal it was argued that this wrongly omitted to mention that being a battered woman was also a relevant characteristic. The Court of Appeal held that the direction as to the attributes of the reasonable person was correct since there was no evidence of such a characteristic raised at the trial, but suggested that had the evidence adduced on appeal been given at the trial 'different considerations may have applied'. Clearly, this leaves open the possibility that post-traumatic stress disorder or 'battered woman syndrome' is a relevant characteristic that can be attributed to the reasonable person.

Interestingly, while Lord Taylor CJ confirmed the decision in *R v Newell* (1980) that permanent or personality characteristics can be attributed to the reasonable person, he conspicuously failed to state that it was only to be done where the provocation was directed at those characteristics. Moreover, the Lord Chief Justice also failed to disapprove the trial judge's direction notwithstanding that the provocation was not directed at the defendant's education or ethnicity. It maybe that the Court of Appeal was signalling its willingness to sever the hitherto requisite link between the defendant's characteristics and the provocation. If this is, indeed, the position it would constitute a significant broadening of the defence of provocation in that the reasonable person could now be attributed with any characteristic, affecting the defendant's power of self-control.

Most importantly, Lord Taylor accepted that the reasonableness of the defendant's conduct cannot be assessed in a vacuum, but had to be considered in the light of the '... history of (her) ... marriage, the misconduct and ill-treatment of the appellant by her husband'. This seems to imply that instead of directing the jury to consider how a reasonable person suffering from 'battered woman syndrome' would have reacted to the provocation (a rather unrealistic thought experiment), the jury can now be asked to simply consider how a reasonable person in the situation of the defendant, who suffered the same level of abuse, would have reacted.

Ahluwalia and diminished responsibility

Although the defendant's lawyers had obtained a psychiatrist's report to the effect that she was suffering from endogenous depression this had not been introduced at the trial. In addition, new material relating to the defendant's mental condition was made available on appeal. Somewhat surprisingly, perhaps, the Court of Appeal exercised its discretion to order a retrial on the ground that an arguable defence of diminished responsibility had been disclosed. At the retrial the judge made it clear that his acceptance of her manslaughter plea was based on diminished responsibility and not provocation. This apparent willingness to accept evidence of diminished responsibility suggests that battered women are likely to evoke a more favourable judicial response if they confine themselves to medical-type excuses rather than the partial justification of provocation.

This aspect of the decision has been subject to much critical comment, not least, from women themselves. This objection has been well put by Donald Nicolson and Rohit Sanghvi ('Battered Women and Provocation: The Implications of *R v Ahluwalia*' (1993) *Criminal Law Review* p 728):

Diminished responsibility ... is more obviously an admission of mental abnormality. Holding it out as the most promising defence for battered women forces them to choose between being labelled as bad or partially mad. Many defendants, like Mrs Ahluwalia herself, might not care as much about their categorisation as about their liberty. But some will undoubtedly perceive it to be deeply insulting to be told that, unless they accept a label of psychological abnormality, they run the risk of escaping the prison of domestic violence only to spend a long time in a less metaphorical prison.

It seems, then, that the decision in *Ahluwalia* has, at least to some extent, enabled the law of provocation to adapt to the situation of the battered woman who kills. It can now be argued that the existence of 'cooling time' will not automatically preclude the defence, particularly where there is a history of provoking acts which cause a 'slow burn' reaction. Moreover, the apparent acceptance of 'battered woman syndrome' both as a characteristic which could be attributed to the reasonable person under the objective limb of the provocation test and as a possible basis for diminished responsibility strengthens the defence position. Unfortunately, this improved defence seems likely to be paid for by defendants having to accept the label of psychological abnormality.

Self-defence as an alternative

Several critics have argued that self-defence more adequately reflects the facts of many cases of battered women who kill and that, if applied to these situations by the judiciary, it would be more likely to result in an acquittal than either provocation or diminished responsibility would be to avoid a murder conviction. Moreover, a plea of self-defence would not necessitate the defendant having to accept the label of mental abnormality in order to improve her chances of acquittal.

According to this view the application of self-defence to the situation of the battered woman who kills would not involve any alteration or extension of the law, but rather an appreciation of the way in which the predicament of the victim fits the existing legal requirements of the defence.

Self-defence can be pleaded at common law and under s 3(1) of the Criminal Law Act 1976 which states that a person may use 'such force as is reasonable in the circumstances in the prevention of crime'. The reasonableness of the defendant's action forms the basis of both defences.

However, the common law of self-defence has developed largely through cases which typically involve male defendants instantly responding to a single violent attack. It is argued that this stereotypical view of the situation where self-defence is relevant, together with the equally stereotypical view of appropriate female behaviour and idealised conceptions of home life, tend to produce a gender-biased concept of reasonableness. It is this rather than any reason of principle or policy which prevents self-defence from accommodating the battered woman who kills.

If the defendant's action is assessed in the context of her situation then killing her partner may, in some cases, be a reasonable course of action. It may be unrealistic, in view of factors such as economic dependence, lack of adequate social welfare and alternative accommodation, the possibility of pursuit and greater injury, the presence of children in the home, to expect the woman to simply leave her abuser. In any case there is no absolute duty to retreat before using force in self-defence (*R v Bird* (1985)). Of course, a willingness to retreat is strong evidence that the defendant is acting reasonably, but the law can hardly require a woman to leave her home and possibly her children before using force to defend herself. Moreover, it would certainly be unreasonable to expect the woman to meekly submit to further violent attacks.

Indeed, the use of lethal force may be reasonable even in situations where there is no immediate threat, perhaps while the man is sleeping or otherwise vulnerable. In an interesting article, Aileen McColgan ('In Defence of Battered Women who Kill' (1993) *Oxford Journal of Legal Studies* p 508) makes this point by means of an analogy with the situation of a hostage:

Where ... someone is held hostage by terrorists who let him know, expressly or by implication, that he is to be seriously injured or killed within the next few days, it is unlikely that the courts would require him to wait until a weapon was actually raised to him before they allowed him to use violence against his captors (...) He cannot be entirely sure that his captors will carry out their threat to kill him, but neither can he reasonably be expected to postpone his use of force until a time when he will most probably not be able to defend himself, given the numerical superiority of his captors or the fact that they are armed and he is not. His only feasible method of escape from the threatened danger might be to seize an opportunity to attack while his captor is asleep or otherwise vulnerable.

Surely, the same is true of a battered woman who fears, probably on the basis of past experience, that a violent attack may soon occur and believes that the alternatives to the use of force such as flight or seeking police protection will be ineffective or temporary.

Although there is undoubtedly a strong case for the application of self-defence to the situation of the battered woman, there seems to be little evidence that judges and defence lawyers have adjusted to this idea (Celia Wells 'Domestic Violence and Self-Defence' (1990) *New Law Journal* p 127).

Infanticide

Criticisms of the existing law

Infanticide is committed when a child under 12 months old is killed by a mother whose mind is disturbed either by reason of her not having fully recovered from the effect of giving birth to the child or by reason of effect of lactation consequent upon the birth of the child (s 1 Infanticide Act 1938). Although infanticide can be raised as a defence to murder, it seems to be more usually charged as a substantive offence in the first place. The maximum penalty is life imprisonment, but most cases are dealt with far more leniently, usually by a probation order (RD Mackay, 'The Consequences of Killing Very Young Children' (1993) *Criminal Law Review* p 21).

Several criticisms can be made of the existing law. First, and, perhaps, most fundamentally, the medical basis of the Infanticide Act 1938 is generally recognised as being psychiatrically unsound. The reference to the effect of lactation appears to be without medical foundation while, in their evidence to the Criminal Law Revision Committee, the Royal College of Psychiatrists acknowledged that social pressures could be just as likely to lead to mental disturbance as any condition linked specifically with the event of giving birth. According to the Royal College, these social pressures could include:

(1) overwhelming stress from the social environment being highlighted by the birth of a baby, with the emphasis on the unsuitability of the accommodation etc;

(2) overwhelming stress from an additional member to a household struggling with poverty;

(3) psychological injury, and pressures and stress from a husband or other member of a family from the mother's incapacity to arrange the demands of the extra member of the family;

(4) failure of bonding between mother and child through illness or disability which impairs the development of the mother's capacity to care for the infant.

The present law, by theoretically limiting infanticide to situations where a direct biological link can be established between giving birth and the imbalance of the woman's mind, ignores the kind of socially induced mental disturbance which would appear to be far more prevalent in practice.

Another criticism is that the statutory definition of infanticide is limited to cases where the mother kills her last born child. In circumstances where the effects of a recent birth cause a mental disturbance which results in the mother killing an older child infanticide will not be available, either as a defence to murder or as an offence in its own right. Here the mother could be liable for murder and yet her culpability is surely the same as if she had killed her youngest child.

Not surprisingly, perhaps, the gender-specific nature of the law of infanticide has also attracted critical comment. It can be argued that males are hardly likely to prove immune from the social and psychological stresses attendant upon childbirth and could well kill while suffering from consequent mental disturbance in exactly the same way as women. Yet the effect of the gender-specific nature of the law, together with the very restrictive biological basis for the mental disorder, operate to unfairly exclude males from the ambit of infanticide. This point would appear to be supported by a statistical analysis conducted by Ania Wilczynski and Alison Morris ('Parents who kill their Children' (1993) *Criminal Law Review* p 21) who concluded that not only were mothers and fathers who killed their children treated differently by the criminal justice system, but also that the mothers were treated more leniently.

Somewhat paradoxically, it can also be argued that the more lenient treatment afforded to mothers who kill their children under the Infanticide Act is insulting to women in that it implies that they are weak characters who 'cave in' to the sort of pressures which the law expects males to withstand. In short, the existing law operates to label female offenders as 'mad' and male offenders as 'bad' and yet both may be reacting to the same sort of pressures with the same degree of culpability.

A final criticism is that there is a disjunction between the rhetoric of the Infanticide Act and the actuality of its operation. For example, research by P d'Orban ('Women who kill their Children' (1979)) indicates that about half of the women who plead guilty to or are convicted of infanticide are not suffering from any identifiable mental disorder at all. There seems little doubt that the Act is often used to introduce covertly socio-economic and other factors in order that offenders receive treatment rather than punishment. It is obviously an unsatisfactory state of affairs when practical action diverges so markedly from legal theory.

Abolition or reform?

Given the strength of the above criticisms it now seems that the principles on which the Act was based are no longer accepted and that mental illness is not now considered to be the only or, indeed, a significant cause of infanticide. In 1975 the Butler Committee recommended the abolition of the separate offence of infanticide on the ground that the defence of diminished responsibility would prove an adequate alternative ('Report of the Committee on Mentally Abnormal Offenders' 1975 Cmnd 6244).

However, the Criminal Law Revision Committee disagreed with the proposal for outright abolition on the ground that, so long as the prosecution are unable to charge manslaughter by reason of diminished responsibility, infanticide has the advantage that it avoids the necessity of charging the mother with murder. In addition it was felt that diminished responsibility might not cover all the circumstances which in practice may be held to justify an infanticide verdict ('Offences Against the Person' 1980 Cmnd 7844). Instead of abolition the Committee recommended extending the existing law of infanticide to cover 'environmental or other stresses'. This suggestion has since appeared in Clause 64(1) of the Criminal Code Bill 1989:

A woman who, but for this section, would be guilty of murder or manslaughter of her child is not guilty of murder or manslaughter, but is guilty of infanticide, if her act is done when the child is under the age of 12 months and when the balance of her mind is disturbed by reason of the effect of giving birth or of circumstances consequent upon the birth.

Although this proposed reform would not address the gender-specific nature of the law, it would go some way towards meeting the other criticisms noted above. It seems a more appropriate measure than outright abolition, particularly if the relatively lenient sentences that women who are subject to high levels of social and psychological stress are to be ensured. Indeed, research has indicated that diminished responsibility under the Homicide Act 1957 is neither widely used in cases which might otherwise be infanticide nor that it could safely cover all cases which presently fall within the ambit of the Infanticide Act 1938 (R D Mackay, 'The Consequences of Killing Very Young Children' (1993) *Criminal Law Review* p 21).

Killing by gross negligence

R v Prentice and Others (1993)

In this case the manslaughter convictions of two hospital doctors who had caused the death of a patient by injecting vincristine into his spine instead of his arm were quashed. At first instance the jury had been directed in terms of *Caldwell* recklessness that the doctors could be convicted if they created an obvious and serious risk of causing serious physical harm and nevertheless went on to take it, or alternatively if they gave no thought to that risk. The Court of Appeal held that this was a misdirection and went back to the rule stated by Lord Atkin in *Andrews v DPP* (1937) that involuntary manslaughter requires gross negligence.

Although critics of *Caldwell* recklessness have generally tended to welcome this reversion to killing by gross negligence as an indication of increasing judicial disquiet with the former decision, there are still criticisms that can be made of it.

Problems with *Prentice*

Lord Taylor stated that (aside from motor manslaughter) the foundation of liability in manslaughter cases involving breach of duty was gross negligence. However, it is not entirely clear what he meant by 'manslaughter cases involving breach of duty'. One interpretation is that he simply meant all cases of involuntary manslaughter other than motor manslaughter (although surely this also involves a breach of duty) and constructive manslaughter. The 'duty', according to this interpretation would be the general duty which human beings owe each other to take care not to harm one another. Alternatively, he could have intended to limit killing by gross negligence to those cases where the defendant owes a more specific duty to take care of the victim's health or safety. This would apply, for example, as in *Prentice* itself, to the risk of harm resulting from medical treatment or work carried out by an electrician.

In addition to the above uncertainty, the decision has been criticised concerning what it is that the gross negligence must relate to. It is clear that there need be no foreseeable risk of death or serious injury, but only of 'risk of injury to health'. This principle originally derives from *R v Stone and Dobinson* (1977), a case involving neglect of a sick relative, and was accepted as sufficient for manslaughter where death unexpectedly results in the present case. However, Glanville Williams has argued that 'injury to health' is too vague a phrase and that the fault element should be as to the risk of causing death, or (in accordance with the *mens rea* of murder), of causing serious injury ('Misadventures of manslaughter' (1993) *New Law Journal* p 1413).

The decision in *Prentice* can also be criticised for leaving the offence of 'motor manslaughter' unaffected. This seems somewhat strange particularly since the argument for the re-emergence of killing by gross negligence was substantially based on the earlier decision in *Andrews v DPP* (1937), itself a motor manslaughter case. There does not appear to be any reason why *Caldwell* recklessness should be preserved for this form of killing, but replaced in relation to other forms of involuntary manslaughter. Of course, it may well be that the Court of Appeal felt it necessary to distinguish 'motor manslaughter' in order to avoid being bound by the decision of the House of Lords in *R v Seymour* (1983) which upheld the *Caldwell/Lawrence* definition of recklessness. Nevertheless, there can be no reason of principle for treating 'motor manslaughter' any differently from other forms, a point explicitly recognised by Lord Roskill in *Seymour*.

A final criticism is that an objective fault requirement like gross negligence is simply inappropriate for such a serious offence as manslaughter. Glanville Williams, in the article mentioned above, argues that the appropriate *mens rea* for involuntary manslaughter should be as stated in Clause 55 of the Law Commission's Draft Criminal Code, namely:

- an intention to cause serious personal harm; or
- recklessness as to whether death or serious personal harm will be caused.

'Recklessness' in this context being defined to mean subjective recklessness of the *Cunningham* type. According to this view putting manslaughter on a basis of subjective recklessness would protect people who through no fault of their own lack the capacity to foresee the relevant risk. In addition, liability would reflect the degree of fault of the offender rather than the extent of the harm caused.

Revision Notes

Non-fatal offences

Common assault

Actus reus
The *actus reus* of an assault consists of causing the victim to apprehend immediate physical violence (*Logden v DPP* (1976)).

It is not clear whether words alone can constitute an assault. In *R v Meade and Belt* (1823) a direction was given to the effect that 'no words or singing could ever constitute an assault', however, in *R v Wilson* (1955), there was an *obiter* statement by Lord Goddard, the Lord Chief Justice, that the phrase 'get out the knives' would, on its own, have constituted an assault.

It is suggested that the better approach is to simply consider whether as a result of the defendant's actions (including his words) the victim feared immediate physical violence. If so, then, surely the *actus reus* of the offence is made out.

There is no doubt that words can negate an assault. In the old case of *Tuberville v Savage* (1669) there was held to be no assault when the defendant reached for his sword and said:

If it were not assize time I would not take such language from you.

Since it was assize time the meaning of this statement was that the defendant was not going to attack the victim. The fear that might have been caused by the conduct of reaching for the sword was negated by the accompanying words.

However, it is suggested that the words must amount to an *unconditional* negation of the fear-inspiring conduct in order to negative any assault.

The courts have sometimes adopted a liberal interpretation of the immediacy requirement in relation to the *actus reus* of common assault. For example, in *Smith v Superintendent of Woking Police Station* (1983) the conviction of a defendant who had frightened a woman by staring through the window of a ground floor flat was upheld. The Division Court found that there was evidence that the victim did fear some immediate violence notwithstanding that the defendant was outside the building at all times.

Mens rea

The *mens rea* for both assault and battery consists of intention or recklessness in causing the victim to apprehend immediate physical violence.

It seems that the relevant recklessness will be of the *Cunningham* rather than the *Caldwell* kind (*R v Savage* (1991)). That is the conscious taking of an unjustified risk of causing someone to fear immediate physical violence.

Common battery

Actus reus

The *actus reus* of a battery consists of the actual infliction of unlawful physical violence.

The degree of 'violence' required is minimal and can consist of the least unauthorised touching of another (*Cole v Turner* (1705)).

Touching a person's clothing will amount to a battery provided the contact is both unauthorised and capable of being felt by the victim (*R v Thomas* (1985)).

The courts presume that people impliedly consent to the normal touching that occurs in everyday life (*Collins v Wilcock* (1984)).

A battery can be inflicted indirectly, for example, by setting a trap for the victim (*DPP v K* (1990)).

Mens rea

As noted above the *mens rea* for both assault and battery is intention or recklessness in the *Cunningham* sense.

Statutory offences

The Divisional Court in *DPP v Little* (1991), found that not only were common assault and battery separate offences, but also that the Offences Against the Person Act 1861 had put them into a statutory form. It is, therefore, no longer correct to refer to them as *common law* assault and battery. They should now be charged under s 39 of the Criminal Justice Act 1988.

Section 47 Offences Against the Person Act 1861

Definition

Section 47 of the Offences Against the Person Act 1861 provides that it is an offence to commit '... any assault occasioning actual bodily harm ...'.

Actus reus

An 'assault' within the meaning of s 47 can consist of either an assault in the technical sense of causing someone to fear immediate unlawful violence, or in the sense of a battery (ie the infliction of unlawful violence).

'Occasioning' means the same as 'causing', therefore, the rules relating to causation will be relevant (see Chapter 1). It will be remembered that the main test for establishing causation in law is to ask whether the result was a reasonably foreseeable consequence of what the defendant was doing.

In *R v Roberts* (1971), Stephenson LJ said that only if the actions of the victim could be shown to be 'daft' would the chain of causation be broken. However, it is sometimes argued that this *dictum* conflicts with the 'thin skull' rule that the defendant must take his victim as he finds him.

It is suggested that there is a difference between a 'daft' victim and a victim who does a 'daft' act. In the former case the victim suffers from a condition of limited intelligence that renders him especially vulnerable and should, therefore, be protected under the 'thin skull' rule. In the latter case the victim is not especially vulnerable, but has engaged in behaviour which is not reasonably foreseeable and which, therefore, breaks the chain of causation.

Actual bodily harm was defined in *R v Miller* (1954) so as to include any hurt or injury likely to interfere with the health or comfort of the victim.

In *R v Chan-Fook* (1993), it was held that actual bodily harm includes psychiatric injury, but does not include mere emotions such as fear, distress or panic.

Mens rea

The *mens rea* is intention or recklessness of the *Cunningham* type. Either of these two mental states need to be established only in relation to the initial assault; it is unnecessary to prove that the defendant intended or foresaw the risk of harm, however slight (*R v Savage* (1991)).

Section 20 Offences Against the Person Act 1861

Definition

Section 20 of the Offences Against the Person Act 1861 creates two offences of '... malicious wounding ...' and '... maliciously inflicting grievous bodily harm ...'.

Actus reus

A wounding requires a complete break of all the layers of the victim's skin (*JCC v Eisenhower* (1984)). Grievous bodily harm simply means 'serious harm' (*R v Saunders* (1985)).

Although most offences under s 20 will involve an assault, it was decided in *R v Wilson* (1983) that 'inflicting' does not necessarily imply an assault. It would seem that if 'inflicting' is to have any meaning at all it is to imply the need for causation.

Mens rea

The word 'malicious' implies a *mens rea* of intention or recklessness of the *Cunningham* type.

The decision of the court in *Mowatt* (1967) placed a 'gloss' on the *Cunningham* definition of recklessness in relation to s 20 in that the defendant is required to have consciously taken an unjustified risk of *some physical harm*, albeit not serious harm.

It follows that foresight that the victim will be frightened is insufficient to found liability in relation to s 20, as stated above, the defendant must have foreseen some physical harm, if only of a minor character (*R v Sullivan* (1981)).

An intention to inflict a wound, not amounting to serious harm, would constitute sufficient *mens rea* for the s 20 offence, but not for the s 18 offence (see below).

Section 18 Offences Against the Person Act 1861

Definition

By s 18 of the Offences Against the Person Act 1861 it is an offence to '... maliciously ... wound or cause any grievous bodily harm ... with intent to do some grievous bodily harm ...'.

Actus reus

The *actus reus* of this offence is exactly the same as that for the s 20 offence and consists of either a wound or grievous bodily harm.

Mens rea

A specific intent to cause grievous bodily harm is required for this offence (*R v Belfon* (1976)).

Sections 23 and 24 Offences Against the Person Act 1861

Actus reus

Both ss 23 and 24 require the administration of a noxious substance.

Whether or not a substance is noxious will depend upon the circumstances in which it is taken. Such circumstances include the quality and quantity of the substance as well as the characteristics of the person to whom it is given (*R v Marcus* (1981)).

'Administering' means causing to be taken, for example, by spraying CS gas into someone's face (*R v Gillard* (1988)).

The *actus reus* of s 23 requires that life must be endangered or grievous bodily harm inflicted as a consequence of the administration of the noxious substance.

Mens rea

Both offences require that the noxious substance be administered intentionally or recklessly in the *Cunningham* sense.

In addition, s 24 requires proof of a further intent to injure, aggrieve or annoy the victim.

Fatal offences

Murder

Actus reus

The *actus reus* of murder is causing the death of a human being within a year and a day (*R v Dyson* (1908)).

A patient kept alive on a life support machine is not regarded as legally dead and is, therefore, capable of being murdered. The original attacker will be held to have caused the death if the machine is turned off as a result of a medical decision made in good faith (*R v Malcherek and Steel* (1981)).

The law of homicide protects the new born child once it becomes capable of independent existence from the mother. There is no need for the umbilical cord to have been cut (*R v Reeves* (1839)), but the child must have been totally expelled from the mother's womb (*R v Poulton* (1832)).

Mens rea

The necessary *mens rea* for murder is an intention to kill or cause grievous bodily harm (*R v Vickers* (1957)).

In cases where it is not clear whether the defendant had such an intention the jury must consider the evidence of what the defendant actually foresaw, and the more evidence there is that he foresaw death or grievous bodily harm as a consequence of his actions, then the stronger the inference that he intended to kill (*R v Hancock and Shankland* (1986)).

In *R v Nedrick* (1986), the House of Lords supplemented the decision in *Hancock* by suggesting that the jury must be satisfied that the defendant foresaw death or grievous bodily harm as a virtual certainty before they could infer intention.

Voluntary manslaughter

There are four particular defences that can operate to reduce a charge of murder to that of manslaughter: provocation, diminished responsibility, suicide pact and infanticide.

Provocation

Section 3 of the Homicide Act 1957 provides:

Where on a charge of murder there is evidence on which the jury can find that the person charged was provoked (whether by things done or by things said or by both together) to lose his self-control, the question whether the provocation was enough to make a reasonable man do as he did shall be left to be determined by the jury; and in determining that question the jury shall take into account everything both done and said according to the effect which, in their opinion, it would have on a reasonable man.

It follows that anything which, as Devlin J said in *R v Duffy* (1949), causes a '... sudden and temporary loss of self-control ...' is capable of amounting to provocation.

In order to establish provocation the jury must decide that:

- the defendant actually lost his self-control; and
- that a reasonable person sharing the same characteristics as the accused, would have lost his self-control in the same circumstances.

The decision of the House of Lords in *DPP v Camplin* (1978) established that the reasonable person should be attributed with the characteristics of the accused, in so far as they are relevant to the provoking words or conduct.

In *R v Newell* (1980), it was held that a characteristic must be not only relevant to the provocation, but also something sufficiently permanent. Thus, intoxication, as distinct from chronic alcoholism, cannot be considered as a characteristic.

In *R v Morhall* (1993), it was held that a self-induced addiction to glue sniffing is not a characteristic attributable to the reasonable person.

Diminished responsibility

Section 2(1) of the Homicide Act 1957 provides:

Where a person kills or is a party to the killing of another, he shall not be convicted of murder if he was suffering from such abnormality of mind (whether arising from a condition of arrested or retarded development of mind or any inherent causes or induced by disease or injury) as substantially impaired his mental responsibility for his acts and omissions in doing or being a party to the killing.

In *R v Byrne* (1960), Lord Parker CJ defined abnormality of mind as '... a state of mind that the reasonable person would find abnormal ...'.

Where the jury has to deal with both diminished responsibility and intoxication, they should first consider whether the defendant would have killed as he did even if he had not been intoxicated. If the answer is 'yes', then, they should go on to consider whether he would have been suffering from diminished responsibility when he did so (*R v Atkinson* (1985)).

However, where it is alleged that the defendant was suffering from diminished responsibility caused by the disease of alcoholism (as opposed to mere intoxication), the jury must try to establish whether the first drink was taken voluntarily – if so the defence will fail (*R v Tandy* (1989); *R v Egan* (1992)).

Suicide pact

Section 4 of the Homicide Act 1954 provides that any killing carried out in pursuance of a suicide pact will be treated as manslaughter rather than as murder.

Infanticide

Section 1(1) of the Infanticide Act 1938 provides that where a woman kills her child before it reaches the age of 12 months, and there is evidence to show that at the time of the killing the balance of her mind was disturbed by the effect of giving birth, then the jury is entitled to find her guilty of infanticide rather than murder.

Involuntary manslaughter

Constructive manslaughter

This offence requires proof that the defendant intentionally committed a dangerous criminal act which resulted in the death of the victim within a year and a day.

The objective nature of the 'dangerous' act was established in *R v Church* (1966), where it was said that:

... the unlawful act must be such as all sober and reasonable people would inevitably recognise must subject the other person to, at least, the risk of some harm ... .

What is meant by 'harm' in this context was clarified in *R v Dawson* (1985) where it was held that the jury must be directed to consider the possibility of *physical* harm as opposed to mere emotional disturbance.

Moreover, the reasonable person should be endowed with all the knowledge that the defendant has gained during the course of the crime (*R v Watson* (1989)).

The illegal act required for constructive manslaughter must be a *criminal* act (*R v Franklin* (1883)), but there is no need for the act to be 'aimed' at the victim in the sense of being intended to do him some harm (*R v Goodfellow* (1986)).

It follows that any act which is both dangerous and criminal will be capable of forming the *actus reus* of the offence. All that is required for the *mens rea* is an intention to do such an act; it is not necessary for the defendant to know that the act is criminal or dangerous (*DPP v Newbury and Jones* (1976)).

Killing by gross negligence

Following the decision of the Court of Appeal in *R v Prentice and Others* (1993) to establish this form of manslaughter the prosecution must prove:

- A duty of care

  It is submitted that the concept of a duty of care, obviously borrowed from the law of tort, is unlikely to prove problematic in the context of criminal law. Surely there is a general duty to take care not to engage in anti-social behaviour?

- Breach of that duty

  The duty not to behave in an anti-social way will be breached whenever there is a reasonably foreseeable risk of injury to health (as opposed to the risk of physical injury required for motor manslaughter – see below) occurring (*R v Stone and Dobinson* (1977)).

- Gross negligence

  According to the Court of Appeal in *R v Prentice and Others* (1993) any of the following states of mind could lead a jury to make a finding of gross negligence:

(a) Indifference to an obvious risk of injury to health.

(b) Actual foresight of the risk coupled with the determination nevertheless to run it.

(c) An appreciation of the risk coupled with an intention to avoid it but also coupled with such a high degree of negligence in the attempted avoidance as the jury considers justifies conviction.

(d) Inattention or failure to advert to a serious risk which goes beyond 'mere inadvertence' in respect of an obvious and important matter which the defendant's duty demanded he should address.

Two of the above four types of gross negligence, (a) and (b) seem to be subjective mental states (in relation to (a), surely you can only be *indifferent* to a result which is foreseen?). Whereas (c) and (d) are clearly objective mental states. However, each case, it seems, is subject to the overriding judgment of the jury: '... gross negligence which the jury consider justifies criminal conviction ...'.

Motor manslaughter

The *actus reus* of this common law offence consists of driving in such a manner as to cause the death of another road user.

Caldwell recklessness, subject to the possible variations suggested by the House of Lords in *R v Reid* (1992), will satisfy the *mens rea* requirements for this offence. The defendant must have either:

- recognised that there was some risk of causing physical injury to another road user, but nevertheless gone on to take it; or
- did not address his mind to the possibility of there being any such obvious risk.

The so called 'lacuna', or gap, in *Caldwell* recklessness occurs where the defendant does consider whether there is a risk and decides that there is none. If this mistaken decision is one that a reasonably competent driver would not have made, then the defendant is not liable for motor manslaughter, but may be liable for the statutory offence of causing death by dangerous driving.

Causing death by dangerous driving

Causing death by dangerous driving, as defined in s 1 and s 2A of the Road Traffic Act 1988, as amended, is, in effect, causing death by grossly negligent driving.

This is because the defendant's driving must fall *far below* the standard of the reasonably competent driver.

It must be obvious to the careful and competent driver that driving in the way that the defendant was actually driving would cause danger of injury to the person or serious damage to property.

5 Offences against property (1)

ESSENTIALS

You should be familiar with the following areas:

- theft, definition, *actus reus* and *mens rea*
- robbery, definition, the meaning of 'force' and 'stealing'
- burglary, building or part of a building, entry, as a trespasser, s 9(1)(a) and (b) definitions
- criminal damage, definitions, *actus reus* and *mens rea*

The *actus reus* of theft

Intangible property

As we will see, the definition of 'property' contained in s 4 of the Theft Act 1968 includes intangible as well as tangible property. The law of theft, therefore, extends to protect such things as the debt owed by a bank to an account holder, either in the form of a bank balance (*R v Kohn* (1979)), or in the form of an agreed overdraft facility (*Chan Man-Sin v R* (1988)). The property which is protected here is not the account holder's money, but the account holder's right to sue the bank for whatever sum is credited, or agreed to be credited to the account. Other forms of intangible property would include patents, copyright, shares, debts, export and other quotas which could be traded for value (*AG for Hong Kong v Nai-Keung* (1988)).

However, for the purposes of theft, there is no property in confidential information, such as business secrets and examination papers (*Oxford v Moss* (1978)). In certain circumstances confidential information is treated as property for the purposes of the civil law and injunctions can be obtained to prevent the disclosure or abuse of such secrets, but there is no criminal liability (*Island Export Finance v Umunna* (1986)). Some commentators have argued, in view of the increasing use and abuse of computerised data-bases, that there is no logical reason why confidential information should not be treated as property for the purposes of the law of theft (eg R Hammond 'Theft of Information' (1987) *Law Quarterly Review* p 252). Others agree that the law should criminalise this kind of property violation, which might be much more serious financially than many of the takings which do fulfil the basic definition of theft, but argue that this is best achieved by further legislation to deal specifically with this kind of property abuse (eg Ashworth 'Principles of Criminal Law' (1991) p 330).

It is the latter approach which has been adopted in the UK with the enactment of the Computer Misuse Act 1990 which creates three offences of unlawfully entering another's computer system with dishonest intent (see M Wasik 'The Computer Misuse Act' (1990) *Criminal Law Review* p 767).

Appropriation by innocent possession and subsequent dishonest intent

Prior to 1968 the law required proof that the defendant had physically taken and carried away the property, a requirement which effectively excluded intangible property such as bank balances from the scope of theft. However, s 3(1) of the Theft Act 1968 adopts a much broader concept of appropriation as 'any assumption of a person of the rights of an owner'. This implies that in some circumstances a simple decision to keep property, unaccompanied by any physical act, could amount to an appropriation. This type of appropriation by omission could occur, for example, where a defendant found property in the street and took it with the intention of handing it in to the police, but later formed the intention to keep it. Similarly, in *Pilgrim v Rice Smith* (1977), a shop assistant who was in lawful possession of goods was held to have appropriated them when she underpriced them and handed them to a friend. The appropriation does not occur until the defendant forms the dishonest intent; it is this mental act which converts what previously had been lawful possession into the *actus reus* of theft.

The *bona fide* purchaser does not appropriate

A *bona fide* purchaser who innocently buys stolen goods and later discovers the truth and decides to keep them might, according to the law as stated above, be guilty of theft. However, special protection for purchasers in good faith is provided by s 3(2) which states:

Where property or a right or interest in property is or purports to be transferred for value to a person acting in good faith, no later assumption by him of rights which he believed himself to be acquiring shall, by reason of any defect in the transferor's title, amount to theft of the property.

The operation of this subsection is well illustrated by the case of *R v Adams* (1993). The defendant had bought motor cycle parts in the belief that they were a 'write off' from a recent accident, in fact they were stolen. He became suspicious two or three days later when he noticed that the engine number had been drilled out. The Court of Appeal quashed his conviction for theft on the ground that the trial judge had failed to direct the jury that the defendant had a defence under s 3(2) of the Theft Act 1968.

As we have seen, the shop assistant who initially is in innocent possession of property, appropriates it by subsequently deciding to underprice it or give it away. However, s 3(2) means that a person who was in good faith at the time he *purchased* the property does not appropriate subsequently by resolving to keep property which he knows he does not own. Of course, if the defendant sold the goods after he learnt that he was not the owner, without informing his buyer of that fact, he could incur liability under s 15 of the Theft Act 1968 for obtaining the purchase price by deception.

Appropriation with consent

As we have seen, the s 3 definition of appropriation as 'any assumption of the rights of an owner' significantly broadened the scope of theft. Indeed, it seems that it has broadened it so far that it even includes acts which the owner of the property consents to. The definition of theft does not include the phrase 'without the consent of the owner', as did the pre-1968 law, and in *Lawrence v MPC* (1972) the House of Lords held that a taking with consent can amount to an appropriation. In this case an Italian student who spoke little English, arrived in England and hired a taxi to take him to an address in London. The proper fare for the taxi journey should have been 52p. The student offered a pound note, the defendant took this and indicated that more was required and took a further £6 from a wallet which was held open for him. Lawrence was convicted of theft and appealed unsuccessfully to the House of Lords.

The defence argument was that there could not have been an appropriation since the victim had consented to the taking of the money.

Viscount Dilhorne rejected this contention and held that the definition of theft does not require the taking to be without the owner's consent. Moreover, it was held that the defendant could appropriate the property at the same time as he became the owner of it.

This decision, which significantly broadened the concept of appropriation to cover cases of consensual taking, not surprisingly, has been the subject of much criticism and controversy. Perhaps the most frequently made point is that the defendant should not have been prosecuted for theft at all, since the case seems to be an obvious one of obtaining property by deception contrary to s 15 of the Theft Act 1968. However, the House of Lords had no power to alter the charge or order a retrial on a different charge, and were understandably reluctant to quash the conviction of a manifestly dishonest defendant. Nevertheless, the theft conviction could have been upheld, without the controversial decision on the irrelevance of consent, on the ground that when the victim offered his wallet he authorised the defendant only to take the correct fare and that in taking more the defendant appropriated by doing what he was not authorised to do.

Appropriation as an unauthorised act

Although *Lawrence* had clearly broadened the concept of appropriation by encompassing consensual taking there followed a series of decisions which incorporated a concept of appropriation which recognised the need for some unauthorised act on the part of the defendant (*R v McPherson* (1973); *Eddy v Niman* (1981) and *R v Skipp* (1975)). For example, in *R v Skipp* (1975) the defendant, who had posed as a haulage contractor, collected three separate loads of produce from London intending not to return to Leicester with them as authorised, but to divert to a new destination and sell them. The question arose as to whether there were one or three appropriations. On appeal it was held that the defendant had been rightly charged with one theft of all the produce. The single appropriation occurred when he diverted from the authorised route with dishonest intent; this was the defendant's first unauthorised act.

This more restricted conception of appropriation received the support of the House of Lords in *R v Morris* (1983). Lord Roskill commenced his judgment by referring to *Lawrence* and re-affirming it as the leading authority on appropriation, but then went on to deliver a speech which appeared to be inconsistent with that earlier decision. The case involved defendants who had switched price labels in a supermarket with the intention of paying a lower price for the goods. In dismissing the appeal, the House of Lords held that the switching of price labels did amount to an appropriation because it was an assumption of the owner's right to determine what price the goods are sold at. Lord Roskill held that the concept of appropriation involved '... not an act expressly or impliedly authorised by the owner but an act by way of adverse interference with or usurpation of those rights.'

It was also made clear that an appropriation occurs when *any* of the rights of an owner had been assumed, there is no need for the prosecution to prove that all the rights of an owner have been usurped.

It seems clear that the concept of appropriation as formulated in *Morris* stands in direct contradiction to that favoured in *Lawrence*. For example, the shopper who takes goods from a supermarket shelf and places them in the trolley provided, with a secret intention to steal, would not appropriate according to *Morris*, since there is no unauthorised act, but would appropriate according to *Lawrence*, since there can be an appropriation even with consent.

The uncertainty created by the contradiction between *Lawrence* and Morris continued for a decade with the courts sometimes following the former precedent (*R v Phillipou* (1989); *Dobson v General Accident Fire and Life Assurance* (1989)) and sometimes the latter (eg *R v Fritschy* (1985)). This unsatisfactory state of affairs finally appears to have been resolved by the decision of the House of Lords in *R v Gomez* (1992) which came down in support of the *Lawrence* concept of appropriation.

The appropriate appropriation?

As we have seen, whether or not an appropriation takes place, where the defendant's acts are consented to by the owner of the property alleged to be stolen, has been a matter of considerable controversy. However, it seems that the issue has been settled, at least for the time being, by the House of Lords. In *R v Gomez* (1992), the defendant was employed as an assistant manager at an electrical goods shop. He sought authorisation from the shop manager to supply electrical goods on the basis of cheques which he knew to have been stolen. The manager instructed him to make enquiries of the bank in order to establish whether the cheques were likely to be honoured. Gomez later told the manager that the cheques were 'as good as cash' and on this basis the goods were supplied. The cheques were eventually returned with an order not to pay because they had been stolen and Gomez was subsequently convicted of two counts of theft.

His appeal to the Court of Appeal was allowed on the ground that the transfer of the goods was '... with the consent and express authority of the owner and that accordingly there was no lack of authorisation and no appropriation'. An approach clearly based on the *Morris* conception of appropriation. The Crown then appealed to the House of Lords.

The appeal was allowed and the convictions were restored. The strict *ratio decidendi* of the case is that there can be an appropriation even if the act in question was expressly or impliedly authorised by the owner, provided that authorisation was produced by fraud or deception. However, the *obiter* statements do not appear to distinguish between consent freely given and consent induced by fraud. This opens up the possibility of a very broad formulation of appropriation in which consent is simply irrelevant, quite irrespective of whether or not is has been induced by any deception. According to this view any interference with property belonging to another, with or without consent, would amount to an appropriation. Of course, whether or not it would amount to theft would depend upon proof of dishonesty and an intention permanently to deprive.

Lawrence was approved of as the foundational authority for the present decision. While the actual decision in *Morris* was said to be correct, statements in the speeches to the effect that an act expressly or impliedly authorised by the owner could never amount to an appropriation were said to be wrong. However, approval was given to Lord Roskill's statement in *Morris* that the assumption by the defendant of *any* of the rights of an owner was sufficient to amount to an appropriation within the meaning of s 3(1). It was also held to be irrelevant to liability under s 1 that the taking did, or might, constitute the offence of obtaining property by deception contrary to s 15 of the Theft Act 1968.

Criticisms of the *Lawrence/Gomez* concept of appropriation

The weight of academic opinion appears to be in favour of the *Morris* conception of appropriation as consisting of an unauthorised act. Several objections can be made to the *Lawrence/Gomez* model of appropriation where consent is irrelevant:

- The absence of the words 'without the consent of the owner' from s 1 of the Theft Act 1968 do not necessarily mean to imply that theft could be committed by an act done with the consent of the owner. As JC Smith notes in his commentary upon the decision in *Dobson* ((1990) *Criminal Law Review* p 274):

The argument is that 'appropriates' was used instead of 'converts' only because it is a word more readily understood by the layman; that it would have been absurd to say 'converts without the consent of the owner' and hardly less absurd to say 'appropriates without consent'; that larceny itself could be committed by conversion as well as by taking without consent; and that larceny by conversion, not larceny by taking, was the model for the Theft Act.

- Since according to *Lawrence/Gomez* there can be an appropriation with the owner's consent and that the defendant can appropriate property while he becomes the owner of it, the distinction between s 1 theft and s 15 deception becomes very blurred. Many cases which would normally be considered as obtaining property by deception would also constitute theft.
- As a result of the decisions in *Lawrence* and *Gomez* the concept of appropriation becomes almost meaningless. In his commentary on *Gomez* ((1993) *Criminal Law Review* p 306) JC Smith writes:

Anyone doing anything whatever to property belonging to another, with or without the authority or consent of the owner, appropriates it: and, if he does so dishonestly and with intent, by that act or any subsequent act, permanently to deprive, he commits theft.

- Since the defendant can appropriate property as he becomes the owner of it there would appear to be no need for the property to belong to another at the time of the appropriation. This further reduces the *actus reus* requirements for theft and, when coupled with a non-pejorative concept of appropriation, reduces the conduct element of the offence almost to vanishing point. Theft, it seems, has become very close to a Orwellian 'thought crime'.

The *Gallasso* case

In *R v Gallasso* (1993), the defendant was a nurse in a home for severely mentally handicapped adults and part of her duties involved looking after the patients' finances. Each patient had a trust account at a building society into which various benefits were paid. Gallasso was the sole signatory and made regular withdrawals for the patients day to day needs. One patient received a cheque for £4,000 which Gallasso paid into a second trust account which she had opened for him. She later transferred £3,000 from the second to the first account and withdrew the remaining £1,000 which she paid into her own account. A few months later another cheque for £1,800 was received and Gallasso opened, on the patients' behalf, a new cash card account at the same building society.

The defendant was charged with three counts of theft; count 1 relating to opening of the second account and the payment in of £4,000, count 2 relating to the payment of £1,000 into her own account and count 3 relating to the opening of the cash card account. She was convicted on counts 2 and 3 (the jury having acquitted her of count 1 as count 2 was charged as an alternative), the court rejecting a submission of no case to answer on count 3, made on the basis that there was no evidence of appropriation on her part.

In allowing her appeal against conviction on count 3, the Court of Appeal was of the opinion that the payment of a cheque into the patient's account could not be regarded as an appropriation since it was evidence of Gallasso affirming the patient's rights rather than assuming them for herself. The court seems to have been swayed by the argument that there must be a *taking* even though it may be with consent and that in this case the payment in '... was not a taking at all'.

Criticisms of *Gallasso*

It is difficult to see how *Gallasso* can be correct as regards the importance the court apparently placed on the need for there to have been a 'taking'. If an appropriation requires a 'taking', cases such as *R v Pitham and Hehl* (1976) would have been wrongly decided and the scope of theft seriously restricted. Such an approach is clearly at odds with the policy of broadening the concept of appropriation adopted by the House of Lords in *Gomez*.

Moreover, the decision seems to imply that not all dealing with property belonging to another will amount to an appropriation, but only that which constitutes an *adverse* interference with the rights of the owner. There are several comments which can be made about this. Firstly, this interpretation is difficult to reconcile with the comments of Lord Keith in *Gomez* which clearly indicate that *any* dealing with property belonging to another would amount to an appropriation. Secondly, there can hardly be an *adverse* interference with the rights of the owner if the owner consents to what is being done. Finally, surely the payment of money into another's account does amount to the assumption of one of the rights of an owner since only the owner has the right to decide which account, if any, that money should be paid into.

It is submitted that *Gallasso* was, for the above reasons, wrongly decided. However, the decision does reflect the unwillingness of the Court of Appeal to fully embrace the broad based and non-pejorative concept of appropriation established in *Gomez*.

All or any of the rights of an owner?

It will be remembered that s 3(1) of the Theft Act 1968 defines an appropriation as any '... assumption by a person of the rights of an owner ...'. Since ownership confers many rights; for example, the right to sell the property, give it away, destroy it, control its physical whereabouts, use it, etc the question arises as to whether it is necessary to assume all or any of these rights for there to be an appropriation. In *Morris*, the House of Lords held that an assumption of *any* of these rights would be sufficient. This aspect of *Morris* was confirmed by the House of Lords in *Gomez*.

Belonging to another at the time of the appropriation

In both *Lawrence* and *Gomez* the defendant obtained property by deception. According to the civil law of contract the ownership of property would pass to the defendant, but the contract would be voidable for fraud. It might, therefore, seem that the defendants in *Lawrence* and *Gomez* would have a defence in that they appropriated their own property, not 'property belonging to another' as required by s 1 of the Theft Act 1968. However, in *Lawrence*, Lord Donovan stated that:

"Belonging to another" in s 1(1) and in s 15(1) in my view signifies no more than that, at the time of the appropriation or the obtaining, the property belonged to another.... .

In *Morris*, Lord Roskill went somewhat further by disapproving of the tendency to try to resolve issues of criminal liability by reference to:

... questions whether particular contracts are void or voidable on the ground of mistake or fraud or whether any mistake is sufficiently fundamental to vitiate a contract. These difficult questions should so far as possible be confined to those fields of law to which they are immediately relevant, and I do not regard them as relevant questions under the Theft Act 1968.

It seems, then, that the courts are prepared to treat the 'belonging to another' requirement as satisfied if the property belonged to another prior to the act of appropriation. If this is a correct statement of the position, the law would seem to run counter to the principle that the *actus reus* and *mens rea* should coincide at the same point in time. However, an alternative interpretation, which goes some way towards avoiding this conflict with principle, would be that the defendant appropriates the property at the same time as he becomes the owner of it.

Moreover, since s 5(1) states that property will be regarded as belonging to any person having in it '... any proprietary right or interest...', it could be argued that the right to avoid a voidable contract falls within these terms. If this is correct then the property would be *regarded* as belonging to another, notwithstanding the passing of a voidable title.

The *mens rea* of theft

Dishonesty

In most cases dishonesty will be unproblematic if the facts alleged by the prosecution are proved and the defendant lacks one of the negating beliefs set out in s 2(1). Normally, therefore, the jury need not be directed as to the legal meaning of 'dishonesty' (*R v Roberts* (1987); *R v Squire* (1990)). However, where there is some doubt, the jury must be directed in accordance with the model direction laid down in *R v Ghosh* (1982).

This direction attempts to achieve a reconciliation between two conflicting lines of authority, one supporting a purely objective concept of dishonesty (eg *R v Greenstein* (1976)) and the other a wholly subjective approach (eg *R v Gilks* (1972)). In *Ghosh*, the Court of Appeal clearly rejected the purely objective approach '... however attractive from the practical point of view that solution may be'. Nevertheless, the court was equally dubious about adopting a wholly subjective approach since this would involve abandoning '... all standards but that of the accused himself, and to bring about a state of affairs in which "Robin Hood would be no robber" '. Instead, the court incorporated both positions in a two-fold test that would be put to the jury.

The first question the jury must answer is the objective one of whether the defendant's actions were dishonest according to the 'ordinary standards of reasonable and honest people'. If the answer to this is yes, then they must go on to consider the subjective question of whether the defendant himself 'must have realised that what he was doing was by those standards dishonest'.

In particular, Lord Lane CJ made it quite clear that a defendant is to be regarded as dishonest even where he believes his actions to be morally justified, if he, nevertheless, realises that ordinary decent people would regard it as dishonest.

Criticisms of the *Ghosh* test

The *Ghosh* approach to the question of dishonesty can be criticised on several grounds. Perhaps, the main criticism is that the test presupposes a wide degree of consensus on what constitutes dishonesty and that, therefore, the term should be treated as an ordinary word. In a multi-cultural and socially stratified society with diverse norms and values what is considered to be dishonest in one segment may be considered acceptable in another. A defendant from a minority subculture could engage in behaviour which he knows would be considered acceptable by the ordinary and decent people of *his* community and yet also realise that it is likely to be considered dishonest by members of the dominant community. The objective limb of the *Ghosh* test, in these circumstances, seems capable of operating in a politically biased way in that members of underprivileged minority groups could be judged by the standards of the relatively wealthy majority. Of course, the strength of this criticism depends on the essentially empirical issue of the degree to which notions of honesty and dishonesty are shared throughout society.

In particular, it is sometimes claimed that the test is likely to result in the criminalisation of some forms of business activity, where the standards of the market-place and the standards of ordinary people might not coincide, ordinary people not being conversant with what is acceptable in the world of business.

On the other hand, if strictly applied, the *Ghosh* test could operate to legitimise many 'dishonest' activities which have become 'acceptable' parts of business and private life. Examples, would include practices such as exaggerating expenses, perhaps with the connivance of employers, in order to reduce taxable earnings, taking and using an employer's property, misleading social security claims and tax declarations etc.

Another objection to using the standards of ordinary decent people as a test for establishing dishonesty is that it will inevitably lead to different results in similar cases (eg Griew 'Dishonesty: The Objections to *Feely* and *Ghosh*' (1985) *Criminal Law Review* p 341). In *R v Feely* (1973), the defendant 'borrowed' money from his employer's safe intending to repay at a later date despite a warning that this practice was prohibited. The Court of Appeal held that the question for the jury should have been whether a person who takes money in those circumstances with an intention to repay an equivalent sum is dishonest according to the standards of ordinary decent people. However, it may well be that different juries would quite sensibly reach different conclusions on this matter. Of course, such inconsistency would not only offend the principle of procedural justice that like cases should be treated alike, but also could effect the efficiency of the criminal justice system by encouraging defendants to plead not guilty in the hope of getting a jury with a flexible view of current standards of honesty.

Finally, there appears to be a possible loophole in the *Ghosh* test in that a defendant may not have thought about whether ordinary decent people would have regarded his actions as dishonest, or even if he had, he may not have been able to form any definite conclusion on the matter.

It is not surprising, in view of the above criticisms of the objective limb of the *Ghosh* test, that some commentators have advocated the adoption of a purely subjective approach. For example, JC Smith (*Law of Theft* (1989) 6th ed) suggests that the test for dishonesty should be 'knowing that the appropriation will or may be detrimental to the interests of the owner in a significantly practical way'. However, as Ashworth ('Principles of Criminal Law' (1991) p 339) has indicated, although the test appears to be subjective:

... in reality the notion of significant and practical detriment would probably become a judgment for the court in all but the rare cases where D could advance a particular explanation for his own belief. In this sense, the proposed test would not cure any tendency of the concept of dishonesty to be a tool used on behalf of wealthy people to convict the poor and members of minority communities ... .

It may be that the *Ghosh* test, even with its inherent difficulties, constitutes a reasonably fair way of establishing dishonesty in the context of a multi-cultural and stratified society.

The intention to permanently deprive

As we have already noted, a permanent deprivation itself is not necessary in order to incur liability for theft, a temporary deprivation will suffice provided there is an *intention* to permanently deprive. Although the Theft Act does not define 'an intention to permanently deprive', it does provide, in s 6, an extended meaning of the concept. The effect of which is that where the defendant's intention is '... to treat the thing as his own to dispose of regardless of the other's rights' he will be deemed to have an intention to permanently deprive. According to Lord Lane CJ in *R v Lloyd* (1985), this means that:

A mere borrowing is never enough to constitute the necessary guilty mind unless the intention is to return the "thing" in such a changed state that it can truly be said that *all* its goodness or virtue has gone. (Emphasis added.)

The use of the word 'all' here means that relatively few borrowings will amount to theft. Presumably if a defendant took a new television set with the intention of returning it in 10 years time, he would not, on Lord Lane's test, be deemed to have an intention to permanently deprive, assuming the television would still be of some value. Similarly, the defendant who takes a season ticket with the intention of returning it one day before it expires would not be liable for theft, whereas he would be if he intended to return it one day after its expiry.

Alternatively, it could be argued that Lord Lane overstates the position somewhat as the actual wording of s 6 – 'in circumstances making it equivalent to an outright taking' – implies that an intention to *substantially* reduce the value of the property would suffice. However, this interpretation would raise the problem of how to assess at what stage something had been 'substantially' reduced in value. Even if certainty could be achieved in this respect, perhaps, by establishing that a 'substantial' reduction implied more than a 50% loss of value, this would still not have adequately addressed the problem. There would be as much difference between the culpability of the defendant who reduced the value of property by 49% and the defendant who reduced it by 51% as there is between the defendant who returned the season ticket one day before expiry and the defendant who returns it one day after. As Ashworth ('Principles of Criminal Law' (1991) p 335) has indicated:

> The real problem here is that there is no general offence of temporary deprivation, and judicial attempts to stretch an offence based on an intention permanently to deprive are likely to produce difficulties.

It is not altogether surprising, therefore, that a strong case has been made for dispensing with the requirement of an intention permanently to deprive altogether (see Glanville Williams, 'Temporary Appropriation Should be Theft' (1981) *Criminal Law Review* p 129). The main argument for criminalising temporary deprivation relates to the fact that the chief value of many items of property lies in the use to which they can be put; the television is mainly of value to us because we can watch it, the lawnmower because we can cut the grass with it etc. Even a temporary loss of such forms of property is significant because we have been deprived of the opportunity to use them for the period of the taking. Indeed, there may be far more gain to the defendant and loss to the victim involved in such temporary deprivations than in an outright theft of other non-functional forms of property.

In addition, it is also argued that such a reform of the law of theft would simplify the existing law by the removal of any need for provisions for the artificial extension of the concept of an intention permanently to deprive. Moreover, it would at the same time pre-empt the need for the creation of further specific offences of temporary deprivation.

Conditional intention to permanently deprive

A conditional intention to permanently deprive the owner of the property is insufficient to satisfy the fault requirements of theft (*R v Easom* (1971)). So, for example, where a defendant takes property with the intention of keeping it if it turns out to be valuable, there will be no liability for theft. A conviction for theft is only possible where there is clear evidence that the defendant had a present intention to permanently deprive. However, the defendant who has a conditional intent to permanently deprive can be convicted of attempting to steal property that he believed to be valuable or in existence since impossibility is no defence under the Criminal Attempts Act 1981 (*R v Shivpuri* (1986)).

Burglary

Entry: the conflict between *Collins* and *Brown*

As we shall see, it is a requirement for both forms of burglary, contained in s 9 of the Theft Act 1968, that the defendant enter a building or part of a building as a trespasser. However, there still seems to be some uncertainty as to precisely what is necessary to constitute an entry and also as to the circumstances in which the defendant will be classed as a trespasser.

Although s 9 replaced the old offences of 'breaking and entering', initially it was assumed that the common law rules relating to entry would continue to apply. Under these rules an entry occurred if the defendant inserted any part of his body into the building or if he inserted an instrument for the purpose of furthering an offence in the building (but not if the instrument was inserted merely in order to gain entry). However, in the leading case of *R v Collins* (1972), the Court of Appeal decided that the entry must be *'effective and substantial'*. Although no express reference was made to the old common law, it is implicit in the judgment that the rule that an insertion of any part of the defendant's body would amount to an entry was rejected. Rather than any definite rule the court appeared to favour a common sense approach to the question of what would constitute an 'effective and substantial' entry in the circumstances of individual cases.

The approach adopted in Collins was modified in *R v Brown* (1985), where the Court of Appeal said that 'substantial' was an unhelpful addition to 'effective' and that the jury ought to be asked only to consider whether the entry was effective. However, this raises the issue of effective in relation to what purpose? In *Brown*, the defendant had been convicted of burglary following evidence that he had lent through a broken shop window with the top half of his body and had rummaged for goods inside. He appealed on the ground that he had not 'substantially' entered a building since half his body had remained outside. Not surprisingly, the conviction was upheld since there was an 'effective' entry as he could easily give effect to his purpose with only half his body inside the shop. This clearly indicates that the effectiveness the court had in mind related to the ulterior offence which he intended to commit in the building, in this case theft of articles in the shop window.

However, if effectiveness must relate to the ulterior offence which the defendant intends to commit in the building, then how could *Collins*, who climbed through a bedroom window with the intention of raping a girl, be said to have made an effective entry *at the moment he stepped over the sill*? An even clearer example is provided by the thief who, intending to steal jewellery from an upstairs bedroom, enters the building by climbing through a downstairs window. He can hardly be said to have made an *effective* entry in relation to the crime he intends to commit as he may be apprehended immediately, the bedroom door might be locked or there might not be any jewellery in the house. It is submitted that a requirement that the effectiveness of an entry must relate to the ulterior offence would substantially and unacceptably narrow the scope of burglary. Smith and Hogan (*Criminal Law* (1992) 7th ed p 615) argue that it would not make any more sense to say that the entry must be effective for the purposes of constituting an entry since such a direction would tend to 'bemuse' a jury. Instead, they suggest that it makes more sense:

... to say that an entry must have been effected and leave it to the jury to decide in a commonsense way whether D is sensibly to be regarded as being outside the building, in the process of entry, or as having entered.

The problem with 'common sense' approaches like this is that they have considerable potential for inconsistency with different juries taking different views on the same facts. However, it is difficult to see how this could be eliminated, even by resort to detailed technical rules, since law is, by its very nature, 'open textured' and capable of different interpretations.

As regards the old common law rules (see above), relating to the insertion of an instrument into the building, there is no direct authority as to whether they have survived the Theft Act. Although Smith and Hogan (*Criminal Law* (1992) 7th ed p 615) point out that there is not the 'slightest hint' of the old distinction between insertion to effect entry (not burglary) and insertion to abstract goods (burglary) in s 9. They go on to suggest that either both should constitute entry for the purposes of burglary or neither should; the latter view being preferable.

Trespass: the conflict between *Collins* and *Jones and Smith*

Just as the decision in *Collins* appears to conflict with that in *Brown*, as regards precisely what the effectiveness of the entry must relate to, so too does it seem to conflict with *R v Jones and Smith* (1976) as to what constitutes a trespass.

In *Collins,* the defendant having climbed a ladder to look through a bedroom window discovered a naked girl asleep on her bed. He then stripped off his clothes, with the exception of his socks (to better equip him to make a rapid escape), and climbed onto the window sill. At this point the girl awoke and, mistaking the defendant for her boyfriend, invited him in. It was only after intercourse had taken place that the girl realised her mistake. A fundamental issue was whether the defendant had entered the building before he was given permission to enter, in which case he had entered as a trespasser, or after, in which case he had not. According to Edmund Davies LJ:

Unless the jury were entirely satisfied that the appellant made an effective and substantial entry into the bedroom without the complainant doing or saying anything to cause him to believe that she was consenting to his entering it, he ought not to be convicted of the offence charged. The point is a narrow one, as narrow maybe as the window sill which is crucial to this case. But this is a criminal charge of gravity and, even though one may suspect that his intention was to commit the offence charged, unless the facts show with clarity that he in fact committed it he ought not to remain convicted.

Clearly, it is not enough that the defendant would be classified as a trespasser in civil law, the criminal offence of burglary requires that he knew, or was at least reckless as to whether he was a trespasser. Equally clearly, and somewhat surprisingly, the Court of Appeal was not prepared to hold that the defendant's alleged conditional intention to rape invalidated the permission to enter.

This latter point stands in sharp contrast with the decision in *R v Jones and Smith* (1976). The defendants entered a house belonging to Smith's father and stole two television sets. They were convicted of burglary contrary to s 9(1)(b) and appealed on the ground that had permission to go into the house and thus could not have been trespassers. Although Smith's father gave evidence to the effect that his son would never be a trespasser in his house, the Court of Appeal upheld the convictions. James LJ applied the reasoning of Lord Atkin in *Hillen and Pettigrew v ICI (Alkali) Ltd* (1936) that a general licence to an invitee:

... only extends so long as and so far as the invitee is making what can reasonably be contemplated as an ordinary and reasonable use of the premises ... he is not invited to use any part of the premises for purposes which he knows are wrongfully dangerous and constitute an improper use.

It followed from this that Smith had entered 'in excess of the permission' given by his father since that permission related to normal domestic purposes and did not extend to theft.

According to the same logic, Collin's entry should have been trespassory since the girl would have hardly invited him in if she had known of his conditional intention to rape her. This conflict between the relatively narrow conception of trespass in *Collins* and the much broader conception in *Smith and Jones* remains to be resolved. Ashworth ('Principles of Criminal Law' (1991) p 345) favours the *Collins* approach on the ground that the essential difference between burglary and theft is that the former often involves fear, threat or an intrusion into the victim's home, making it a far more serious offence. Where the person who enters has a general permission to do so these 'aggravating' features are unlikely to be present and so, in these circumstances, the more appropriate offence would one of theft.

Implications of *Smith and Jones*

It is, perhaps, worth noting some of the implications that the broad conception of trespass contained in *Smith and Jones* would have in a shopping context. A person who enters a shop with an intention to steal (or rape, cause grievous bodily harm or criminal damage) inside would commit a s 9(1)(a) burglary at the moment of entry. If he then picked up any item with the *mens rea* of theft (ie dishonesty and an intention permanently to deprive), not only would he commit a s 1 theft, but simultaneously a s 9(1)(b) burglary. If, however, the defendant formed the intention to steal after he had entered the building, he would not be liable for either form of burglary, unless he entered *part* of the building (eg the area behind the counter or a storeroom) with that intention.

Conditional intention

We noted earlier in this chapter that a conditional intention permanently to deprive someone of property is insufficient to sustain a charge of theft (*R v Easom* (1971)). However, in relation to burglary under s 9(1)(a) a conditional intention to steal, rape, cause grievous bodily harm or criminal damage will suffice (*AG's Reference No 1 and 2 of 1979* (1979)).

Revision Notes

Theft

Definition

The basic definition of theft is to be found in s 1(1) of the Theft Act 1968 which provides that a person who:

... dishonestly appropriates property belonging to another with the intention of permanently depriving the other of it ...

is guilty of theft.

Actus reus

Property
Section 4(1) of the Theft Act 1968 defines 'property' as:

... money and all other property, real or personal, including things in action and other intangible property.

This seemingly all encompassing definition is subject to both common law and statutory exceptions. The following do not constitute property:

- information (*Oxford v Moss* (1979));
- electricity (*Low v Blease* (1975));
- a human corpse (*R v Sharpe* (1857));
- land (s 4(2));
- wild plants (s 4(3));
- wild animals (s 4(4)).

However, there are also some exceptions to the exceptions rendering some of the above capable of being stolen in certain circumstances:

- a human corpse does become property capable of being stolen if skill or effort has been exercised on it (*Doodeward v Spence* (1907)): moreover, products of the body such as blood and urine are capable of being stolen (*R v Rothery* (1976); *R v Welsh* (1974));
- land can be appropriated by (a) a trustee, personal representative or liquidator, (b) someone not in possession can appropriate anything that is severed from the land, and (c) a tenant can appropriate any fixture (s 4(2)(a),(b) and (c));
- wild plants can be stolen if the whole plant is taken or the plant is taken for sale or reward (s 4(3));

- wild animals can be stolen if they are tamed or ordinarily kept in captivity or have been, or are in the process of being, reduced into another's possession (s 4(4)).

Belonging to another

The basic definition of 'belonging to another' is contained in s 5(1) of the Theft Act 1968:

Property shall be regarded as belonging to any person having possession or control of it, or having in it any proprietary right or interest ... .

Thus, in *R v Turner No 2* (1971) an owner was convicted of theft of his car when he removed it from a garage where it was undergoing repairs without informing the proprietor. Since the garage had possession and control the car was treated as if it belonged to another in accordance with s 5(1).

The above case is often contrasted with that of *R v Meredith* (1973) where it was held that a car owner who had removed his vehicle from a police pound could not be guilty of appropriating his own property. As the police clearly had control of the car the decision is difficult to reconcile with *Turner* and is, perhaps, best regarded as wrongly decided.

Section 5(3) of the Theft Act 1968 extends the meaning of 'belonging to another':

Where a person receives property from or on account of another, and is under an obligation to the other to retain and deal with that property or its proceeds in a particular way, the property or proceeds shall be regarded (as against him) as belonging to the other.

As the 'obligation' must be legally enforceable (*R v Gilks* (1972)), this will normally involve either contractual obligations or obligations imposed under a statute.

The terms of the contractual or statutory duty must be examined in order to establish the precise nature of the obligation. If the defendant is permitted to do what he likes with the property, his only obligation being to account in due course for an equivalent sum, s 5(3) does not apply (*R v Hall* (1973)). However, the defendant need not be under an obligation to retain particular monies; it is sufficient that he is under an obligation to keep in existence a fund equivalent to that which he has received (*Lewis v Lethbridge* (1987)).

Section 5(4) covers the situation where the defendant receives property by mistake:

Where a person gets property by another's mistake, and is under an obligation to make restitution ... then ... the property or proceeds shall be regarded (as against him) as belonging to the person entitled to restoration ... .

If the mistake is fundamental the subsection is not of relevance as no property can pass under a void contract. Where the mistake is non-fundamental the contract will be voidable, but even in these circumstances, it can be argued that the subsection is not relevant as there is no obligation to make restoration until the contract is actually avoided.

However, it seems that in certain situations the prosecution are able to argue that property belongs to another, either under a straightforward application of s 5(1), or via s 5(4):

- mistaken overpayment of wages (*AG's Reference No 1 of 1983* (1984));
- mistaken crediting of a bank account (*R v Shadrokh-Cigari* (1988)).

In addition, it is thought that the subsection would apply to situations where the defendant receives too much change or too many goods by mistake.

Appropriation

Appropriation is defined in s 3(1) of the Theft Act 1968 as 'any assumption by a person of the rights of an owner ...'.

Appropriation can, therefore, take many forms, including:

- offering the property for sale (*R v Pitham and Hehl* (1976));
- taking the property;
- pledging the property;
- destroying (although not damaging) the property;
- fixing the price of the property (*R v Morris* (1983)).

In *R v Gomez* (1993), the House of Lords decided that any interference with property belonging to another would amount to an appropriation, irrespective of whether the owner consented or authorised the act in question. However, as *Gomez* was a case where consent had been obtained by fraud, the strict ratio would seem to be that there can be an appropriation even though there is consent provided the consent is obtained by fraud or deception.

Mens rea

Dishonesty

There is a negative definition of dishonesty set out in s 2(1) of the Theft Act 1968. A person is not dishonest if he appropriates in the honest belief that:

- he has a legal right to deprive another of the property (s 2(1)(a));
- he would have the other's consent if the other knew of the appropriation and the circumstances of it (s 2(1)(b));

- the person to whom the property belongs cannot be discovered by taking reasonable steps (s 2(1)(c)).

A positive test for establishing dishonesty was laid down by the Court of Appeal in *R v Ghosh* (1982). In cases of doubt the jury should be given the following direction:

Was the defendant dishonest according to the standards of ordinary decent people? If yes, did the defendant realise that what he was doing was dishonest by these standards?

Intention permanently to deprive

In the vast majority of cases it will be obvious whether or not the defendant had an intention permanently to deprive the other of the property at the moment of appropriation. However, in two situations the defendant will be deemed to have such an intention to permanently deprive:

- if it is his intention '... to treat the thing as his own to dispose of regardless of the other's rights: and a borrowing or lending of it may amount to so treating it if, but only if, the borrowing or lending is for a period and in circumstances making it equivalent to an outright taking or disposal' (s 6(1)); or
- where he parts with property '... under a condition as to its return which he may not be able to perform ...' (s 6(2)).

In relation to s 6(1) the intention permanently to deprive will only be deemed to exist if the defendant intended to return the goods in a fundamentally changed state so that virtually all of their value would have been lost (*R v Lloyd* (1985)).

Robbery

Definition

Section 8(1) of the Theft Act 1968 provides that:

A person is guilty of robbery if he steals, and immediately before or at the time of doing so, and in order to do so, he uses force on any person or puts or seeks to put any person in fear of being then and there subjected to force.

Actus reus

Force

As can be seen from the above definition the Act requires proof of either the use or the threat of force against the person. Whether force actually has been used or threatened is a matter for the jury to decide (*R v Dawson* (1976)).

The force can be used or threatened against any person, not necessarily the owner of the property (*Smith v Desmond Hall* (1965)).

It is clear that the force, or threat of force, must be used in order to steal and not for any other reason (*R v Shendley* (1970)).

Moreover, the use of force, or threat of force, must occur before or at the time of stealing. The use of force even seconds after the appropriation has taken place would not amount to robbery. However, the courts have been prepared on some occasions to hold that an appropriation could consist of a continuing act (*R v Hale* (1978)).

Stealing

All the elements required for s 1(1) theft are necessary to establish that the defendant has stolen for the purposes of robbery. Thus, in *R v Robinson* (1977), the defendant's conviction for robbery was quashed on the basis that since he honestly believed that he was entitled to the property in question he was not dishonest under s 2(1)(a) and, therefore, incapable of committing theft.

Burglary

Definitions

Section 9 of the Theft Act 1968 creates two burglary offences.

Section 9(1)(a)

By section 9(1)(a) a person is guilty of burglary if '... he enters any building or part of a building as a trespasser ...' with an intention to:
• steal;
• inflict grievous bodily harm;
• rape;
• commit unlawful damage to the building or anything therein.

Section 9(1)(b)

A person is guilty of this offence if having entered a building or part of a building as a trespasser he commits or attempts to steal, or inflict grievous bodily harm.

Actus reus

Both burglary offences require that the defendant has entered a building or part of a building as a trespasser.

Building or part of a building

There is no complete definition of what constitutes a 'building' contained in the Act. The following points should be noted in this respect:

- inhabited vehicles or vessels will amount to a 'building' for the purposes of the Act, even when the inhabiting person is not there;
- in *Stevens v Gourley* (1859), it was stated that a building was '... a structure of considerable size and intended to be permanent or at least to endure for a considerable length of time';
- in *B and S v Leathley* (1979), a large freezer container without wheels and which was connected to the electricity supply was held to constitute a building;
- in *Norfolk Constabulary v Seekings and Gould* (1986), a lorry trailer with wheels, used for storage and connected to the electricity supply, was not held to be a building;
- in *R v Walkington* (1979), a customer who went behind a till counter was held to have entered part of a building as a trespasser.

Entry

Section 9 requires that the defendant must enter, or have entered, a building or part of a building. In *R v Collins* (1972), it was held that an entry must be 'effective and substantial'.

In *R v Brown* (1985), a case which involved the defendant leaning through a broken shop window, it was held that the crucial word in the *Collins* test was 'effective' and that 'substantial' did not materially assist in the matter. As the defendant was able to reach the articles he wished to steal his entry was held to be 'effective' and the conviction was upheld.

As a trespasser

The defendant must not only enter a building, he must do so as a trespasser. A trespasser is someone who enters property without express or implied permission.

A defendant who has permission to enter for particular purposes, but then exceeds the express or implied conditions of entry, will enter as a trespasser. For example, in *R v Smith and Jones* (1976) the defendants had permission to enter the house of Smith's father for normal domestic purposes, but not in order to steal the television set.

The defendant must know or be reckless in the *Cunningham* sense as to whether his entry is trespassory (*R v Collins* (1972)).

Criminal damage

Definitions

Section 1(1)
This subsection provides that the 'basic' offence of criminal damage is committed where:

A person who without lawful excuse destroys or damages any property belonging to another intending to destroy or damage any such property or being reckless as to whether any such property would be destroyed or damaged.

Section 1(2)
This subsection states that an 'aggravated' offence is committed where:

A person who without lawful excuse destroys or damages any property, whether belonging to himself or another:

(a) intending to destroy or damage any property or being reckless as to whether any property would be destroyed or damaged; and

(b) intending by the destruction or damage to endanger the life of another or being reckless as to whether the life of another would be thereby endangered.

Section 1(3)
This subsection provides that where property is destroyed or damaged by fire, the offence is charged as arson and is punishable with a maximum sentence of life imprisonment.

Actus reus

Property
Property is defined in s 10(1) as anything of '... a tangible nature, whether real or personal, including money ...'.

Although somewhat similar to the definition of 'property' provided in s 4 of the Theft Act 1968 it should be noted that criminal damage can be committed in relation to land, while land cannot be stolen, conversely intangible property can be stolen, but cannot be the subject of criminal damage.

Belonging to another

The property must belong to another for the purposes of s 1(1) criminal damage, but need not belong to another in relation to the s 1(2) offence.

Property will be treated as 'belonging to another' for the purposes of s 1(1) if that other has custody or control of it or has any proprietary right or interest in it or has a charge on it (s 10(2)).

Damage

Whether property has been destroyed or damaged will depend upon the circumstances of each case, the nature of the article and the way in which it is affected. The following cases provide illustrations of acts which were held to have amounted to criminal damage:

- in *Blake v DPP* (1993), a biblical quotation written on a concrete pillar with a marker pen was held to amount to criminal damage;
- similarly, in *Hardman and Others v The Chief Constable of Avon and Somerset Constabulary* (1986), the spraying of human silhouettes by CND supporters on pavements was held to constitute damage notwithstanding that the figures would be washed away by the next rainfall;
- in *Roe v Kingerlee* (1986), it was held that the application of mud to the walls of a cell could amount to damage as it would cost money to remove it;
- the unauthorised dumping of waste on a building site, which cost £2,000 to remove, was held to constitute criminal damage in *R v Henderson and Battley* (1984);
- in *Samuel v Stubbs* (1972), criminal damage was held to have been done to a policeman's helmet when it had been jumped upon causing a 'temporary functional derangement'.

The following two cases illustrate actions which were not held to have amounted to criminal damage:

- in *A (a juvenile) v R* (1978), a football supporter who spat on a policeman's coat was found not to have committed criminal damage since the coat did not require cleaning or other expenditure;

- a scratch caused to a scaffolding bar did not amount to criminal damage in *Morphitis v Salmon* (1990) since its value or usefulness was not impaired.

Mens rea

The 'basic' s 1(1) offence

The *mens rea* required for the basic offence of criminal damage is an intention to do an act which would cause damage to property belonging to another or being reckless, in the *Caldwell* sense, in relation to such an act.

The 'aggravated' s 1(2) offence

The *mens rea* for this more serious form of criminal damage consists of an intention to damage property and an intention that the damaged property endanger life, or recklessness, in the *Caldwell* sense, as to whether this occurs.

There is no need for life to actually be endangered, all that is required is that the defendant *intended* the damage to endanger life, or was reckless as to whether this occurred (*R v Dudley* (1989)).

However, the defendant's *mens rea* as to whether life is endangered must extend to the consequences of the criminal damage, and not be limited merely to the act causing the damage. For example, in *R v Steer* (1980), the defendant's conviction under s 1(2) for firing rifle shots at the windows of his victims house was quashed on appeal. There was no evidence that he intended or was reckless as to whether the broken glass, as opposed to the shots themselves, would endanger life.

Defences

Honest belief in the owner's consent

Section 5(2)(a) provides that a person will have a lawful excuse if:

... he believed that the person or persons whom he believed to be entitled to consent to the destruction of or damage to the property in question has so consented, or would have so consented to it if he or they had known of the destruction or damage and its circumstances.

Defence of property

Under s 5(2)(b) the defendant will have a lawful excuse if, in order to protect property, he damaged other property provided he believed that the property was in immediate need of protection and that the means of protection were reasonable in the circumstances.

Section 5(3) clearly provides that the defendant's belief that his actions are reasonable does not itself have to be reasonable. However, the courts have sometimes appeared reluctant to judge defendants on the basis of what they considered to be reasonable in the circumstances (see *Blake v DPP* (1993)).

6 Offences against property (2)

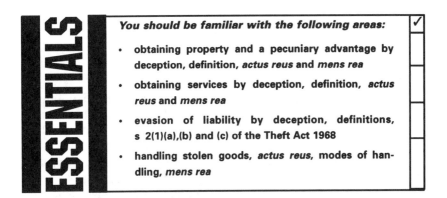

You should be familiar with the following areas:

- obtaining property and a pecuniary advantage by deception, definition, *actus reus* and *mens rea*
- obtaining services by deception, definition, *actus reus* and *mens rea*
- evasion of liability by deception, definitions, s 2(1)(a),(b) and (c) of the Theft Act 1968
- handling stolen goods, *actus reus*, modes of handling, *mens rea*

Common elements

As we have seen, following the decision of the House of Lords in *R v Gomez* (1992), the distinction between theft and deception has become rather blurred. It seems that virtually all cases of obtaining property by deception could now be prosecuted as theft, although the reverse is not true as there are many ways of appropriating property that do not involve a deception. The crucial difference between the two offences, which has been undermined, is that, in relation to the deception offences, the owner of the property voluntarily parts with it following a deception by the defendant.

All the deception offences contained in this chapter share four elements in common. These elements are:

- there must be a deception;
- the deception must be 'operative' in that it must cause the obtaining of:
  (a) property (s 15 Theft Act 1968)
  (b) pecuniary advantage (s 16 Theft Act 1968)

(c) services (s 1 Theft Act 1978)

(d) remission of a liability (s 2(1)(a)Theft Act 1978)

(e) waiting or forgoing a payment (s 2(1)(b) Theft Act 1978)

(f) exemption from or abatement of liability (s 2(1)(c) Theft Act 1978);

- the defendant must intend or be reckless as to whether he deceives;
- the defendant must be dishonest.

These four common elements will be considered in turn.

Deception

The essence of deception is '... to induce a man to believe that a thing is true which is false' *(per* Buckley J, in *Re London and Globe Finance Corporation Ltd* (1903)) and s 15(4) of the Theft Act 1968 makes it clear that this can occur as a result of words or conduct.

Deceptions may be express, where the prosecution must prove that the statement is untrue, or implied, where it is necessary for the prosecution to prove that the defendant intended (or is reckless whether) his words and conduct to imply an untruth to the victim. It is not enough for the prosecution merely to show that certain facts may be reasonably inferred from the defendant's words and conduct.

Examples of implied representations by conduct include the person who writes a cheque (impliedly representing that he has an account at the issuing bank and that the cheque will be paid) and the motorist who fills his car with petrol at a service station (impliedly representing that he will pay). Moreover, it seems clear that there is a duty to undeceive in circumstances where a representation which was true when it was made, becomes false prior to the obtaining. In *DPP v Ray* (1974), the House of Lords held that a person who enters a restaurant and orders a meal is impliedly representing by his conduct that he will pay. The defendant in this case did intend to pay, but later discovered that he had insufficient funds to cover the bill and remained silent as to this change in circumstances. He continued the representation by remaining seated until the waiters left the dining area unattended and then ran out without paying. It was held that the very fact of remaining in the restaurant and continuing to behave as a *bona fide* customer amounted to a misrepresentation and, therefore, a deception.

Similarly, in *R v Firth* (1990), the failure of a consultant to comply with his contractual duty to inform the Area Health Authority as to whether patients referred by him to a NHS hospital were private patients was held to be a deception.

However, it is worth noting that both *DPP v Ray* and *Firth* were not cases involving mere silence. In the former case there was conduct and in the latter there was a contractual duty to act. There is, therefore, no direct authority under the 1968 Act as to whether silence, or to put it another way, an omission to undeceive, can amount to a deception.

Although most deceptions will consist of representations of fact, s 15(4) makes it clear that a deception as to law will suffice. A possible example of this would be where a dishonest lawyer informs his client that he is under a legal obligation to make certain payments when he is not.

What cannot amount to a deception is a mere statement of opinion, although distinguishing between fact and opinion can be problematic. If the defendant knows of facts which contradict what he saying, then there will be a deception even if the statement is expressed in the form of an opinion. For example, in *R v King* (1979), a defendant who knew the recorded mileage of a car to be inaccurate committed a deception by stating that 'it may be incorrect', since this implied that as far as he knew it was accurate. On the other hand, the car salesman who knowingly exaggerates the merits of a car by asserting that it is 'a good runner' is unlikely to commit the offence of deception since the courts have tended to adopt a lenient approach on the basis that 'puffs' of this kind are unlikely to deceive anyone (*R v Bryan* (1857)).

A defendant who makes a statement, which he believes to be untrue, but which unknown to him is truthful is not liable for any deception offence since there is in reality no deception. Thus, in *R v Deller* (1952) the defendant induced the victim to purchase a car by stating that it was free from encumbrances. The defendant had previously executed a document which purported to mortgage the car to a finance company, however, unknown to him, this transaction was void for technical reasons. Strange as it may sound, he had dishonestly told the truth when he said that the car was free from encumbrances and, therefore, had not deceived the purchaser. Nevertheless, it should be remembered that in situations like this the defendant will almost certainly have taken steps which he believes are more than merely preparatory to obtaining property by deception and could consequently be convicted of attempting to obtain property by deception contrary to s 1 of the Criminal Attempts Act 1981.

The deception must be operative

In order to secure a conviction under ss 15 and 16 of the 1968 Act or ss 1 and 2 of the 1978 Act the prosecution must prove not only that there was a deception, but also that the deception *operated* to enable the defendant to obtain the property, pecuniary advantage, service or evasion of liability. In other words, the deception must have preceded the obtaining and must have *caused* the victim to obtain the property, services etc. If the victim is not affected by the deception, none of these offences will be committed, even though the obtaining is allowed to take place (*R v Hensler* (1870)).

In most cases where there is an express deception the normal rules for establishing causation can be applied (see Chapter 1). In *R v Laverty* (1970), a case involving the sale of a stolen car, the alleged deception was that the car did not bear its original number plates. However, the answer to the 'but for' test – but for this deception would the defendant have obtained the purchase price? – was yes, indicating a nonoperative deception. The victim bought the car because he believed the defendant was authorised to sell it and there was no evidence to show that he would have minded that the car did not bear its original plates. If the alleged deception had been that the defendant represented that he was authorised to sell the car then this might well have amounted to an operative deception.

Somewhat more problematic are the cases where there is a deception implied by conduct. In these cases the courts seem prepared to adopt a somewhat broader concept of causation. This approach is illustrated by the case of *MPC v Charles* (1977), where the defendant had purchased gambling chips at a casino by using his cheque card to cash cheques to a total value of £750. The House of Lords held that there was a deception since this conduct impliedly represented that the defendant had the bank's authority to use the cheque card to this extent. In fact the defendant had grossly exceeded his agreed overdraft limit of £100 and, therefore, clearly lacked such authority. Having determined that there was a deception, the next step was to establish that it was operative in the sense that it caused the obtaining of the cash and it is at this point that the judgment becomes controversial.

In evidence the casino manager stated that he was prepared to cash the cheques because he knew that payment would be made by the bank. This tends to suggest that the defendant's deception did not cause the obtaining in that it did not operate on the victim's mind. It seems that it was the bank's guarantee of payment which caused the manger to cash the cheques rather than the defendant's implied representation that he had authority to use the card. On the other hand, the manager had also stated that he would not have cashed the cheques if he had known that the defendant was not authorised to use the cheque card to that extent. Somewhat surprisingly, in view of the evidence, the

House of Lords held that the victim had accepted the cheques because he was deceived by the defendant into believing that the defendant had authority to use the card.

Similarly, in *DPP v Ray* (1974), as we have already noted, a customer in a restaurant made a continuing representation that he would pay by the very act of remaining at the table, eating food, and ordering coffee. Adopting the approach, outlined above, the House of Lords held that this deception was operative in the sense that if the waiter had known of the defendant's change of mind, then it is extremely unlikely that he would have left him alone. Of course, this is not causation in the direct sense that the waiter left the room because he assumed that the defendant's original representation that he would pay remained unchanged.

As Ashworth has noted, the causation test which the courts apply in these cases is not one of *actual* causation, but one of *hypothetical* causation ('Principles of Criminal Law' (1991) p 352). According to this broader test, the question is not whether the defendant's deception actually operated on the victim's mind causing him to part with the property, but whether the victim would have acted in the same way if he had known the true position. The fact that in reality the victim did not know, and did not take any steps to discover, the truth is irrelevant.

This hypothetical test of causation has been criticised on the ground that it is inconsistent with the legislature's use of the concept of deception. According to the Criminal Law Revision Committee the term 'deception' can be distinguished from 'fraud' or 'false pretences' in that it emphasises the effect that the offender actually produced in the mind of the person deceived (8th Report 1966 para 87). Yet decisions such as those discussed above effectively negate this requirement. Another criticism is that the hypothetical test conflicts with established principles in so far as it deviates from the need to establish an 'operative and substantive' cause (ATH Smith 'The Idea of Criminal Deception' (1982) *Criminal Law Review* p 721).

These cases can be understood as embodying a conflict between the principles of causation, as traditionally understood, and the policy of widening the net of criminal liability in order to convict culpable defendants, even in circumstances when the alleged misrepresentation was never actively considered as a reason for action by the victim. Clearly, social defence policy reasons have proved powerful enough to draw the courts away from both the traditional doctrine of causation and the intention of the legislature.

Intention/recklessness as to deception

Section 15(4) of the Theft Act 1968 makes it clear that the prosecution must prove, as part of the requisite *mens rea* for obtaining property by deception, that the defendant intended to deceive or was reckless as to whether he deceived. Section 16(3) incorporates the same requirement in relation to the offence of obtaining a pecuniary advantage, while s 5(1) of the Theft Act 1978 incorporates it in relation to offences under ss 1 and 2 of that Act.

Although there is no direct authority on the point, there seems to be a consensus among the academic commentators, given the subjective element in dishonesty, that *Caldwell* recklessness cannot apply to deception offences. This is because it seems rather improbable that a defendant could have failed to realise that there was an obvious risk that he might be deceiving another and yet at the same time have realised that his conduct would be considered dishonest by the standards of ordinary people. It is submitted that recklessness in relation to the deception offences involves more than simple negligence on the part of the defendant and must amount to the conscious taking of an unjustified risk of deceiving someone. There is some support for this position which favours the adoption of *Cunningham* recklessness, in relation to the deception offences, to be found in the judgments in *R v Staines* (1974) and *Large v Mainprize* (1989).

It follows that a defendant may be convicted not only where he knows that what he represents is virtually certain to be untrue, but also where he is aware that his representation may or may not be true.

Dishonesty

Unlike dishonesty in relation to theft, to which s 2(1) applies, there is no negative definition of dishonesty expressly provided in relation to the deception offences. However, the Criminal Law Revision Committee have indicated that this omission was in order to avoid unnecessary legislative complications and that:

... a person who uses deception in order to obtain property to which he believes himself entitled will not be guilty; for though the deception may be dishonest, the obtaining is not

(Cmnd 2977 para 88).

It appears, in line with theft, that an honest belief in a legal right to deprive an owner of property, or obtain a pecuniary advantage, service or evasion of a liability will, despite the absence of a negative definition

124

of dishonesty, nevertheless operate as a defence.

In other cases the *Ghosh* direction should be given to the jury where there is some doubt as to dishonesty.

Use of cheques and cheque/credit cards

The defendant's own account

Where a defendant issues a cheque there is an implied representation that the cheque will be honoured on presentation. In *R v Gilmartin* (1983), Lord Goff LJ stated this principle in the following terms:

... by the simple giving of a cheque, whether post-dated or not, the drawer impliedly represents that the state of facts existing at the date of delivery of the cheque is such that in the ordinary course the cheque will on presentation for payment on or after the date specified in the cheque, be met.

Of course, the represented 'state of affairs' mentioned by Lord Goff is that there are sufficient funds in the account, or that sufficient funds will be paid in before the cheque is presented, or that there is an agreed overdraft facility to cover the cheque.

In *MPC v Charles* (1977), the use of a cheque card has been held to impliedly represent not only that the bank will meet the cheques, but also that the defendant has the authority to use the cheque card. Similarly, in *R v Lambie* (1981) it was held that the use of a credit card implies not only that the credit card company will pay the relevant sum to the retailer, but also that the defendant has the authority to use the credit card for the purpose in question.

It is clear from the above cases that the use of a cheque book, cheque or credit card all involve implied representations to the effect that payment will be made on the due date. Moreover, as we have already seen, the courts are prepared to treat the issue of whether these representations are operative as unproblematic.

It follows that a defendant who issues a cheque (unsupported by a cheque card), knowing that there are insufficient funds to cover it in his account, would incur liability for obtaining property by deception from the retailer, contrary to s 15 of the 1968 Act, or possibly services contrary to s 1 of the 1978 Act. Since the bank would be unlikely to honour the cheque in these circumstances there would be no possibility of liability for either theft or obtaining a pecuniary advantage by deception from the bank.

Where the defendant issues a cheque supported by a cheque card, knowing that there are insufficient funds in the account, there would, once again, be liability in relation to obtaining property or services by deception from the retailer contrary to s 15 of the 1968 Act or s 1 of the 1978 Act respectively. However, since the bank is contractually bound to honour the cheque in these circumstances, the defendant would also commit an offence under s 16 of the 1968 Act, by obtaining a pecuniary advantage (being allowed to borrow by way of overdraft) by deception. The fact that the deception is exercised on the retailer and the pecuniary advantage is obtained from the bank would not affect liability.

Whether the defendant would also be committing theft against the issuing bank is somewhat more problematic. In *R v Navvabi* (1986), the defendant had been convicted of theft having drawn cheques on his account, supported by a cheque card, when there were insufficient funds to cover them in the account. The Court of Appeal quashed his conviction on the ground that the defendant's use of the cheque and cheque card merely gave the payee a contractual right to payment as against the bank. It followed that there was no assumption of the bank's rights in relation to its funds either at the time the cheque was made out, or at the time the payment was made. It would appear from this judgment that the payment of money by the bank to the payee could only be regarded as an appropriation if the bank was directly authorised by the defendant. In this case the bank made the payment to the payee because of the contractual obligations arising as a result of the use of the cheque card, and not because it wished to respond to the defendant's instructions.

However, one point made in *R v Morris* (1984) and confirmed in *R v Gomez* (1992) was that an appropriation could consist of the assumption of *any* one of the rights of an owner. Following from this, it could be argued that one of the rights of an owner is to determine precisely when contractual obligations with a third party will arise and that by the unauthorised use of a cheque supported by a cheque card the defendant had assumed this right.

In relation to the use of a credit card, in excess of an agreed spending limit, there will, once again be liability for obtaining property by deception, contrary to s 15, as against the retailer. However, as it seems somewhat strained to regard a credit card account as an overdraft facility, a charge of obtaining a pecuniary advantage by deception contrary to s 16 would be inappropriate. Another possibility, since most credit card companies now make a charge for their services, would be a charge of obtaining services by deception contrary to s 1 of the Theft Act 1978.

Another's account

Where a defendant takes another's cheque book and forges the signature of the account holder he will be liable for obtaining property or services by deception as against the retailer contrary to s 15 of the 1968 Act or s 1 of the 1978 Act. Here the defendant makes an implied representation not only that the cheque will be honoured, but also that he is the person entitled to draw the cheque. In addition, to the deception offences he will also incur liability under the Forgery and Counterfeiting Act 1981.

Another possible offence would be theft against the account holder rather than obtaining a pecuniary advantage by deception against the bank since the defendant can hardly have obtained an overdraft facility in these circumstances.

It is clear that the contents of a bank account, or an overdraft facility, can constitute property belonging to another for the purposes of the law of theft (*R v Kohn* (1979)). However, it seems equally clear that where a defendant makes an unauthorised use of a cheque book, in respect of an account which is not in credit and has no overdraft facility, there cannot be a theft, simply because there is no property to steal. Of course, in these circumstances a charge of attempted theft would be more appropriate.

In view of the point made in *Morris*, and approved in *Gomez*, to the effect that an appropriation could consist of the assumption of any of the rights of an owner, it seems that the drawing, presenting or negotiating of forged cheques would amount to an appropriation (*Chan Man-Sin v R* (1988)). The fact that the account holder would lose nothing, since the bank only has authority to pay the valid cheques of its customers and, therefore, would be contractually bound to credit his account with the amount wrongly paid out on the forged cheque, would be irrelevant here. Only the account holder has the right to make out cheques on his account and it is this right which is assumed by the defendant.

Another, rather unlikely, possibility would be a charge of theft in relation to the cheque itself. The obvious defence argument here would be that since the cheque can be returned to the account holder once it has been processed through the banking system there is unlikely to be an intention permanently to deprive on the part of the defendant. This argument was considered in *R v Duru* (1973), where it was held that a cheque is a chose in action which undergoes a fundamental change in legal status once it has been processed through the banking system. Since it is returned to the account holder only after it has been cashed, virtually all of its value has been lost and the defendant can, therefore, be deemed to have an intention permanently to deprive the owner of it under s 6 of the Theft Act 1968.

However, where by deception the victim is induced to write a cheque in favour of the defendant, the situation appears to be entirely different. Professor JC Smith has argued that in these circumstances the cheque, as a thing in action, as opposed to a mere piece of paper, never constitutes 'property belonging to another' (*Law of Theft* (1989) 6th ed p 139, see also commentary on *R v Mitchell* (1993) *Criminal Law Review* p 789). The key point here is that the right to payment belongs, from the moment the cheque is written, to the defendant. It follows that the cheque, in its capacity as a thing in action, is incapable of being obtained by the defendant, in his capacity as payee, by deception because it is already his. If there is no property belonging to another there can be neither an obtaining of it by deception nor an appropriation of it.

Support for the above position is provided by the decision in *R v Danger* (1857). In this case a defendant was found not guilty of obtaining a valuable security by false pretences when he had induced the victim to accept a bill of exchange, signed by himself as drawer and made payable to himself. It was held that to be the subject of obtaining by false pretences there must be property belonging to someone other than the accused. The victim had no property in the document, in its capacity as a valuable security, because the thing in action belonged to the defendant.

It can also be argued, in these circumstances, that theft of the cheque in its capacity as a piece of paper is equally untenable since there is no intention permanently to deprive. The argument that the cheque undergoes a fundamental change of status as a result of being processed through the banking system and that the defendant, under s 6(1), can be deemed to have an intention permanently to deprive, is only of relevance in relation to theft of the cheque in its capacity as a thing in action. As a result of the cheque being processed through the banking system, the person who has been permanently deprived of the thing in action is not the victim, but the defendant. The cheque did not have any value to lose from the moment it was written from the point of view of the victim as it was the means by which his bank account would be depleted. It was only of value, as a thing in action capable of being transformed into cash, to the defendant.

Moreover, it can hardly be a convincing argument that the cheque, in its capacity as a piece of paper, has undergone a loss of all or substantially all of its value when it is returned to the victim having been processed by the bank. After all, it lost any value it had as a blank cheque form when the victim wrote it out in favour of the defendant. Since, it could not be used again for that purpose, it's only value appears to be as a record of a transaction concerning the defendant's account, but it's value in this respect has not been impaired at all.

JC Smith suggests that the least unsatisfactory way of justifying a conviction for obtaining a cheque by deception is by the court inferring a conditional intention permanently to deprive. This seems a reasonable approach since if the defendant knew that the cheque had been stopped, or was not going to be honoured for some other reason, then he would not present it. In these circumstances it is extremely unlikely that he would have an intention to return the cheque to the victim, more probably he would simply not care what happened to it and would throw it away or otherwise dispose of it. However, this solution only appears to encompass rather artificial charges relating to the cheque as a piece of paper.

To summarise the above argument, where the defendant obtains a cheque made out to himself by deception, there is no liability either in relation to s 15, where there is an intention permanently to deprive, but the property does not belong to another, or in relation to theft of the cheque, as a piece of paper, where the property does belong to another, but where there is no intention permanently to deprive. Similarly, on the basis of the above argument, a charge of theft from the account of the drawer would not be sustainable since the cheque, as a thing in action, will not have constituted property belonging to another from the outset.

Revision Notes

Obtaining property by deception

Definition

Section 15(1) of the Theft Act 1968 provides:

A person who by any deception dishonestly obtains property belonging to another, with the intention of permanently depriving the other of it, shall ... be liable ... .

Actus reus

Property belonging to another
Section 34(1) provides that s 4(1) and s 5(1) relating to property belonging to another should apply generally for the purposes of the Act. The concepts of 'property' and 'belonging to another', therefore, have a similar meaning to that already noted in relation to s 1 theft (see Chapter 5).

Obtaining
Section 15(2) provides:

For the purposes of this section a person is to be treated as obtaining property if he obtains ownership, possession or control of it and "obtains" includes obtaining for another or enabling another to obtain or to retain.

Clearly, the *actus reus* of the offence will be committed where the defendant induces the victim to sell, give or loan property. However, it seems that the offence would not be committed where the defendant by deception is allowed to retain property of which he already had possession or control. The appropriate charge in these circumstances would be one of theft, by virtue of s 3(1).

However, following the decision in *R v Gomez* (1993), that consent is irrelevant to appropriation, there would now seem to be a large area of overlap between s 1 and s 15.

Deception
Section 15(4) provides:

For the purposes of this section "deception" means any deception (whether deliberate or reckless) by words or conduct as to fact or as to law, including a deception as to the present intentions of the person using the deception or any other person.

Obviously, to constitute a deception the statement must be untrue (*R v Deller* (1952)). Moreover, a statement of mere opinion cannot amount to a deception.

A deception can only work on a human mind so a machine cannot be deceived (*Davies v Flackett* (1972)).

Clearly, conduct can amount to a deception (*DPP v Ray* (1974)).

Causation

The deception must be operative in the sense that it must cause the obtaining of the property. It follows that the 'but for' test and other rules relating to causation, noted in Chapter 1, are relevant to deception.

In *R v Collis-Smith* (1971) the defendant, having filled his car with petrol, falsely told a garage attendant that his employer would pay. On appeal it was held that the deception could not have been operative since it was not made until *after* the property in the petrol had already passed to the defendant. The appropriate charge in these circumstances would have been under s 2 of the 1978 Theft Act (see below).

Mens rea

The *mens rea* for the s 15 offence consists of three elements:

* intention or recklessness (in the *Cunningham* sense) in relation to the deception;
* dishonesty;
* intention to permanently deprive.

Both the *Ghosh* test and the s 6 provisions relating to an intention to permanently deprive apply to the s 15 offence. However, the s 2(1) negative definitions of dishonesty do not apply.

Obtaining a pecuniary advantage by deception

Definition

Section 16(1) of the Theft Act 1968, as amended, provides:

A person who by any deception dishonestly obtains for himself or another any pecuniary advantage shall ... be liable ... .

Actus reus

The deception must cause the obtaining and 'deception' and 'obtaining' have the same meaning as for s 15 above.

'Pecuniary advantage' does not include any financial benefit, but is limited to the following very specific situations:

- being allowed to borrow by way of overdraft;
- taking out a policy of insurance or annuity contract, or obtaining an improvement of the terms on which the defendant is allowed to do so;
- being given an opportunity to earn remuneration or greater remuneration;
- being given the opportunity to win money by betting.

Mens rea

The requisite *mens rea* consists of two elements:

- intention or recklessness (of the *Cunningham* type) in relation to the deception;
- dishonesty.

   The *Ghosh* test as to dishonesty can be given in cases of doubt.

Obtaining services by deception

Definition

Section 1(1) of the Theft Act 1978 provides:

A person who by any deception dishonestly obtains services from another shall be guilty of an offence.

Actus reus

A 'service' is broadly defined in terms of a 'benefit' that an individual would be willing to pay for (s 1(2)).

   'Deception' has the same meaning as in relation to s 15 of the 1968 Theft Act and must be operative in the same way (s 5(1)).

Mens rea

The mental element for this offence consists of an intention or recklessness (in the *Cunningham* sense) in relation to the deception and dishonesty. Once again, in cases of doubt concerning dishonesty the *Ghosh* direction should be given to the jury.

Evasion of liability by deception

Definitions

Section 2(1) of the Theft Act 1978 creates three offences of evasion of liability by deception. It would appear that the three offences are not mutually exclusive (*R v Holt* (1981)). The offences are committed where a person by deception:

(a) dishonestly secures the remission of the whole or part of any existing liability to make a payment, whether his own liability or another's; or

(b) with intent to make permanent default in whole or in part on any existing liability to make a payment, or with intent to let another do so, dishonestly induces the creditor or any person claiming payment on behalf of the creditor to wait for payment (whether or not the due date for payment is deferred) or to forgo payment; or

(c) dishonestly obtains any exemption from or abatement of liability to make a payment ... shall be guilty of an offence.

Actus reus

As is common to all the deception offences, the deception must be operative in that it must cause the securing of the remission of liability.

The 'liability' must be an existing legal liability to pay with the exception of s 2(1)(c) which encompasses future liabilities (*R v Frith* (1990)).

It would appear that the words 'secured the remission' of the liability in s 2(1)(a) denote nothing less than the total extinguishing of the legal liability to pay. However, it can be argued, as a matter of civil law, that an existing liability can never be extinguished by a deception. This is because any agreement to extinguish liability will be rendered void, or at least, voidable, by deception and, therefore, will not be totally extinguished. If this argument is correct, it is difficult to see how anyone could ever be liable in relation to s 2(1)(a).

Notwithstanding the above argument, in *R v Jackson* (1983) the Court of Appeal upheld the defendant's conviction under s 2(1)(a) for using a stolen credit card to pay for petrol and other goods.

Mens rea

The *mens rea* common to all three offences under s 2, is that the defendant should be dishonest and intend to deceive or be reckless, in the

Cunningham sense, as to whether he deceives. In addition, for the s 2(1)(b) offence there must also be an intention to make permanent default, in other words an intention never to pay the debt.

Making off without payment

Definition

Section 3(1) of the Theft Act 1978 provides:

... a person who, knowing that payment on the spot for any goods supplied or service done is required or expected from him, dishonestly makes off without having paid as required or expected and with intent to avoid payment of the amount due shall be guilty of an offence.

Actus reus

The offence will not be committed if the payment is not legally enforceable or where the supply of goods or the doing of the service is contrary to law (s 3(3)).

It seems that for the offence to be complete the defendant must have 'made off' by leaving the premises where payment is due (*R v McDavitt* (1981)).

Failing to pay includes leaving an inadequate amount, counterfeit notes or foreign currency. It would also include using another's cheque or credit card or leaving a cheque that will be dishonoured.

Mens rea

The defendant must know that payment on the spot is required and intend to permanently avoid payment and to be dishonest.

Handling stolen goods

Definitions

Section 22(1) of the Theft Act 1968 provides:

A person handles stolen goods if (otherwise than in the course of stealing) knowing or believing them to be stolen goods he dishonestly receives the goods, or dishonestly undertakes or assists in their retention, removal, disposal or realisation by or for the benefit of another.

Some of the key terms used in this section are themselves subject to further statutory definition. For example, s 34(2)(b) states that 'goods' include:

... money and every other description of property except land, and includes things severed from the land by stealing.

From this definition it would appear that choses in action, such as a bank account into which money obtained in exchange for stolen property has been paid, will constitute stolen goods (*R v Pritchley* (1973); *AG's Reference No 4 of 1979* (1980)).

In addition, s 24(4) makes it clear that in order to constitute stolen property the goods must have been obtained as a result of theft, obtaining property by deception, or blackmail.

However, goods will lose their 'stolen' status if they are restored to the person from whom they were stolen or to other lawful possession or custody (s 24(3)). Thus, in *Haughton v Smith* (1975) tins of meat ceased to be 'stolen' when police took control of the lorry transporting them.

What constitutes 'custody' seems to depend on the degree of control exercised over the goods. For example, in *AG's Reference No 1 of 1974* (1974) the Court of Appeal were unwilling to hold that a police officer who immobilised a car, that he suspected of containing stolen goods, by removing its rotor arm had taken custody of the property.

In a situation where goods have ceased to be 'stolen', because they have been taken into lawful custody, a defendant who handles them in the belief that they are stolen could be liable for attempting to handle stolen goods contrary to s 1(1) of the Criminal Attempts Act 1981.

It should be noted that where the stolen goods have been exchanged for other forms of property, that other property may also constitute 'stolen goods'. Section 24(2) provides that for goods to be stolen they must be, or have been, in the hands of the thief or handler and directly or indirectly represent the stolen goods in whole or in part.

For example, if a stolen picture is exchanged for cash and the cash then used to buy a car; the picture, the cash and the car are all stolen goods.

Actus reus

Modes of handling

Receiving
Taking possession of the stolen property. It is not necessary to show that the defendant acted 'for the benefit of another'.

Removal
Moving the stolen goods from one place to another. The transportation must be 'for the benefit of another'.

Realisation
Selling or exchanging the stolen goods. The realisation must be 'for the benefit of another.'

Disposal
Destroying or hiding the stolen goods. The disposal must be 'for the benefit of another'.

Retention
Keeping possession of the stolen goods. The retention must be 'for the benefit of another'. It seems that a mere omission to inform the police of the presence of stolen property will not amount to retention (*R v Brown* (1970)), however, in *R v Kanwar* (1982), a defendant who deliberately misled the police as to the presence of stolen goods in her home was held to have assisted her husband in their retention.

As well as the above five modes of handling, it is also an offence to arrange to do any of these things or to assist in the removal, realisation, disposal or retention of stolen goods by another person (s 22(1)).

For the benefit of another
All of the above modes of handling, with the exception of receiving and arranging to receive, require that the defendant act 'for the benefit of another'. It follows that a defendant who knowingly sells stolen goods for his own benefit will not be liable for arranging, assisting or undertaking the realisation of stolen property. The innocent purchaser would not be 'another person' within the meaning of the subsection (*R v Bloxham* (1983)).

Otherwise than in the course of stealing
The above words, included in the definition of the offence, are necessary to prevent many instances of theft from automatically becoming handling as well. Despite the decision of the Court of Appeal in *R v Pitham and Hehl* (1977), it would seem that the phrase 'course of stealing' clearly implies a continuous rather than an instantaneous act. However, such a continuous act concept entails obvious uncertainties about precisely when the act commences and terminates. The practical solution is to allow the jury to decide this matter on a case by case basis.

Mens rea

There are two elements to the *mens rea* of handling: dishonesty and knowledge or belief that the goods are stolen.

In relation to dishonesty, the *Ghosh* test can be applied in cases of difficulty, but should not be automatically resorted to (*R v Roberts* (1987)).

A belief that the property is stolen is a purely subjective matter and should not be equated with what the reasonable person would have believed in the same circumstances (*Atwal v Massey* (1971)).

Where there is evidence that should have made the defendant suspect that the goods were stolen, the jury are entitled to infer a belief that they were stolen (*R v Lincoln* (1980)). However, mere suspicion is not to be equated with such a belief (*R v Grainge* (1974)).

In the absence of a satisfactory explanation to the contrary, a jury is entitled to infer a belief that the property is stolen where there is evidence that the defendant came into possession of the goods soon after the theft.

7 General defences

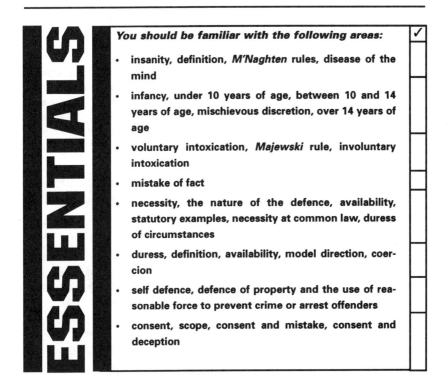

Intoxication

The compromise between principle and policy

The existing law relating to voluntary intoxication can be criticised as representing an unsatisfactory compromise between principle and policy. This compromise can be clearly identified in the decision of the House of Lords in *DPP v Majewski* (1977), where their lordships acknowledged the fundamental principle that criminal liability requires the formation of a mental element by allowing intoxication negating *mens rea* as a defence to offences of specific intent. However, they were also influenced by policy objectives in allowing conviction for basic intent offences despite intoxication preventing the formation of the requisite mental element.

Several of the judges in *Majewski* explicitly accepted that the decision was unsatisfactory in that it did not comply with accepted theory. Lord Salmon noted '... that there is a degree of illogicality in the rule that intoxication may excuse or expunge one type of intention and not another', while Lord Edmund Davies not only acknowledged the contradictory nature of the decision, but also clearly indicated the policy of social defence which produced it:

Illogical though the present law may be, it represents a compromise between the imposition of liability upon inebriates in complete disregard of their condition (on the alleged ground that it was brought on voluntarily), and the total exculpation required by the defendant's actual state of mind at the time he committed the harm in issue. It is at this point pertinent to pause to consider why legal systems exist. The universal object of a system of law is obvious – the establishment and maintenance of order ...

Therefore, in the case of voluntary intoxication, the usual principles of responsibility do not apply, at least in relation to offences of basic intent.

A compromised compromise?

One attempted justification of the admittedly 'illogical' decision in *Majewski* is that specific intent offences require proof of intention, which the defendant may lack as a result of intoxication, whereas basic intent offences are those that can be committed recklessly. Although a defendant charged with a basic intent offence may not be subjectively reckless at the time the harm was caused, as a result of intoxication, he is deemed to have been reckless at the time he became intoxicated. This is because everyone is assumed to know the risks involved in taking alcohol and 'dangerous drugs'.

Several objections can be made in relation to this argument. An obvious point is that the objective recklessness involved in becoming intoxicated effectively replaces the subjective recklessness required for many crimes of basic intent. Moreover, this objective recklessness does not relate to the risk of the harm specified in the definition of the offence in question, but simply relates to the risk of becoming intoxicated. In addition, because the defendant is deemed to be reckless at the time of becoming intoxicated rather than at the time the offence is committed, the *Majewski* rule conflicts with the general principle of contemporaneity; that the *actus reus* and the *mens rea* must exist at the same point in time.

An alternative, more subtle, justification was suggested by the court in *R v Woods* (1981), where it was held, in relation to basic intent offences, that the jury should discount the fact that the defendant was intoxicated and consider whether, if the defendant had been sober, he would have foreseen the risk in question. According to this approach, a defendant would not be deemed to be reckless simply by becoming intoxicated, indeed, the drunken defendant could be acquitted of a basic intent offence if the jury accepts that he would have lacked the necessary *mens rea* for the offence had he been sober. This argument seems to have the support of The Law Commission (Consultation Paper No 127 (1993) para 3.20) and Glanville Williams (*Textbook of Criminal Law* (1983) 2nd ed).

However, the approach suggested in *Woods* is open to the very persuasive objection that it expects the impossible of jurors by requiring them to ignore the actual facts and engage in crystal ball gazing in order to try to discover what the defendant would have foreseen if he had not been intoxicated. It is submitted that this is a fiction which is likely to mask the application of objective recklessness under a subjective guise.

In the case of offences of basic intent which require a *mens rea* of *Caldwell* recklessness the impact of *Majewski* is somewhat reduced. Where the defendant gave no thought to the existence of the risk, whether as a result of intoxication or some other reason, he would be liable even without the rule in *Majewski*. This is because *Caldwell* recklessness consists of the conscious or unconscious taking of an obvious risk. As we have seen, where the defendant did consider whether there was a risk and mistakenly decided that there was none, he would normally have a good defence (*R v Reid* (1992)). However, the present law can be further criticised in that if the mistaken decision that there was no risk was made in an intoxicated state, then the effect of *Majewski* is to close the 'loophole'.

Without doubt, the most telling criticism of the existing law is that evidence of intoxication in relation to a crime of basic intent effectively converts that crime into an offence of strict liability. This is because the prosecution will be relieved of their duty of proving *mens rea* beyond reasonable doubt once evidence of intoxication has been introduced. Not only does this allow convictions for serious offences effectively without *mens rea*, but also conflicts with the principle that the prosecution have the burden of proving the mental element for the crime in question (*Woolmington v DPP* (1935)).

Another criticism of the *Majewski* rule is that it is only capable of partially achieving the policy objective of social protection, in that there are a number of specific intent offences which cannot be reduced to lesser, basic intent offences. In these cases intoxication will provide a complete defence and the drunken 'offender' will escape conviction. Indeed, even in relation to those specific intent offences with a lesser included basic intent offence, it can be argued that a conviction for the lesser offence does not accurately reflect the defendant's real culpability.

In view of the above criticisms it seems that there is a strong case to the effect that the present law, in relation to intoxication does not accord with the accepted principles for establishing criminal liability, is illogical, unethical and unnecessarily complex. Moreover, the policy objective of securing convictions for those causing harm while intoxicated is not always achieved. In short, the attempted compromise between principle and policy embedded in the *Majewski* decision is ultimately unsatisfactory and the case for reform by the legislature compelling.

The Law Commission's proposals for reconciling policy and principle

Having accepted the unsatisfactory nature of the existing law and following a consideration of several possible alternatives, The Law Commission have provisionally concluded that the *Majewski* rule ought to be abolished (Law Commission Consultation Paper No 127 'Intoxication and Criminal Liability' (1993)). Instead, evidence of intoxication should be taken into account by the jury in deciding whether the defendant acted with the requisite *mens rea* and in deciding whether the defendant held an excusing belief or acted in an autonomic state.

The effect of this proposal would be to resolve many of the contradictions of principle created by the *Majewski* decision and to greatly simplify the law. A defendant would be acquitted if on the evidence, including evidence of intoxication, he lacked the *mens rea* for the crime in question. However, as Graham Virgo has argued, in his article 'Reconciling Principle and Policy' ((1993) *Criminal Law Review* p 415), such an approach fails to preserve the acknowledged policy of *Majewski* that, intoxicated defendants ought to be punished, if only for reasons of public safety. Moreover, he also makes the pragmatic point that both public and Parliament are unlikely to look favourably on the simple abolition of the *Majewski* distinction. It is, perhaps, for these reasons that The Law Commission further proposed that consideration be given to the creation of a new offence of 'criminal intoxication'.

Similar proposals have been made before by both the Butler Committee in 1975 (Committee on Mentally Abnormal Offenders) and by a minority of the Criminal Law Revision Committee in their examination of the law of offences against the person. The essence of The Law Commission's proposals is to impose liability for the new offence on any person who committed the *actus reus* of one of a number of listed offences (most involving personal violence or damage to property, but excluding attempts and offences involving dishonesty), while awareness, understanding or control was substantially impaired by deliberate intoxication, whether or not the *mens rea* of the specified offence was absent. The Law Commission argued that since punishment should be related to the harm caused, but should also be less than that for the completed offence, the maximum sentence should be two-thirds that for the specified offence.

The proposed abolition of the *Majewski* rule, together with the creation of the new offence of causing harm while intoxicated, have been welcomed by Graham Virgo as '... the ideal solution for reconciling the conflicting demands of principle and policy in respect of offenders who are intoxicated'.

The triumph of principle over policy: the Australian solution

A far more radical solution to the ethical uncertainty and illogicality of the *Majewski* rule has been adopted by the High Court of Australia and the New Zealand Court of Appeal. In the Australian case of *O'Connor* (1981) and the New Zealand case of *Kamipeli* (1975) it was held that self-induced intoxication may be relied upon to support a denial of *mens rea* irrespective of the type of offence charged, thus abolishing the *Majewski* distinction without replacing it with any new offence. This approach represents the triumph of principle over policy rather than any attempt to reconcile the two. As such it has much to commend it; simplifying a complex area of law while paying due regard to the reality of the defendant's mental state at the time of the offence.

It has been argued by Gerald Orchard in his article 'Surviving without *Majewski* – A View from Down Under' that the Australian approach would be preferable to The Law Commission's provisionally preferred solution, involving the abolition of the *Majewski* distinction and the creation of a new offence of criminal intoxication ((1993) *Criminal Law Review* p 426). In particular, he questions whether a new offence is necessary in order to achieve the policy objective of social defence.

In both Australia and New Zealand acquittals as a result of intoxication raising doubt as to the required state of mind are 'very unusual'. This is because, as Gerald Orchard points out:

... while intoxication may often contribute to and explain intentional offending it will seldom result in the absence of the modest mental requirements of intention, awareness and foresight that generally suffice for *mens rea*.

Indeed, in the New Zealand case of *Kamipeli* (1975), it was said that it would often be necessary to warn a jury that absence of *mens rea* as a result of intoxication 'is a conclusion not to be lightly reached'. Moreover, it was accepted that the judge could direct the jury to ignore the issue of intoxication negating the requisite mental state if there was insufficient evidence to support this conclusion. In short, the policy of social defence would appear to be well served by ordinary principles of subjective liability and does not require additional buttressing by the creation of a new offence.

In addition to the above argument that the creation of a new offence is unnecessary from the standpoint of policy, Orchard also makes the point that it would be unsound on grounds of principle:

While it is common knowledge that intoxication may lead to aggressive and dangerous behaviour, there will be cases where neither the individual's experience nor the circumstances of the intoxication suggest any real risk of this. In such a case it is suggested that even gross voluntary intoxication does not involve such a degree of culpability as to justify criminal liability.

The argument against the creation of a new offence of criminal intoxication is, thus, a two-pronged one of principle and policy. Voluntary intoxication negating *mens rea* is a conception of fault which is too broad to justify conviction for serious offences, especially if there is no good reason for supposing that it will achieve the policy of social defence any more effectively than ordinary principles of liability.

Mistake and self defence

Wrong turnings in the law?

Some commentators have argued that the law of mistake, in relation to self-defence and the use of reasonable force in the prevention of crime or the arrest of offenders, under s 3 of the Criminal Law Act 1967, appears to have followed an unsatisfactory line of development.

For example, AP Simester ('Mistakes in Defence' (1992) *Oxford Journal of Legal Studies* p 295) argues that the principle in *DPP v Morgan* (1976), that a mistaken belief must be honest, but need not be reasonable, was wrongly applied in *R v Williams (Gladstone)* (1984) and *Beckford v R* (1988) to self-defence situations. This argument proceeds by drawing attention to the distinction between defences which consist of a denial of *actus reus* or *mens rea* and those which do not deny the *prima facie* offence, but seek to excuse it by reference to the circumstances in which it occurred. Automatism would be an example of the first kind of defence, whereas self-defence, necessity and duress would be examples of the second, supervening, type of defence.

It is then argued that this distinction was understood and accepted by the House of Lords in *Morgan*, where the non-consent of the victim was said to constitute the *actus reus* of rape. Thus, the principle, that a mistake need not be reasonable as long as it is honest, is only of relevance to mistakes which have the effect of negating *actus reus* or *mens rea* and not to supervening defences such as self-defence where a belief in the necessity for violence must be reasonable. Indeed, in *Morgan*, Lord Edmund Davies expressly acknowledged that the law '... requires reasonable grounds for believing that physical action in self-defence or the defence of another is called for'.

Morgan misunderstood?

However, the Court of Appeal in *Williams* and the Judicial Committee of the Privy Council in *Beckford* interpreted *Morgan* as if it had fundamentally altered the law in this respect. The following passage taken from the judgment in *Beckford* indicates how the principle in *Morgan* was applied to self-defence situations as if this was a logical necessity:

If then a genuine belief, albeit without reasonable grounds, is a defence to rape because it negates the necessary intention, so also must a genuine belief in facts which if true would justify self-defence be a defence to a crime of personal violence because the belief negates the intent to act unlawfully.

As Simester points out, by ignoring the distinction between defences which deny the essential elements of an offence and those which excuse, this statement masks a moral proposition under the guise a logical conclusion.

Should an unreasonable mistake constitute self-defence?

Of course, one can accept that the decision in *Morgan* does not provide direct authority for the application of a subjective concept of mistake in the context of self-defence while at the same time maintaining that it ought to. Glanville Williams ('Offences and Defences' (1982) *Legal Studies* p 233) argues that it would be illogical to require mistaken defences to be reasonable in relation to supervening defences while there is no requirement for them to be reasonable in relation to the offence elements. There is, he claims, no sensible distinction between a person who shoots his wife, believing her to be a rabbit, and a person who shoots his wife, believing her to be a burglar. However, Simester disagrees, noting that killing another person is *prima facie* wrongful, and that a defendant will know that he ought to be very sure of having good reasons for doing so before embarking on such a drastic course of action. On the other hand, where a defendant believes that he is engaging in conduct which is *prima facie* lawful it is quite a different matter.

A step too far?

As we have seen, it can be argued that the extension of the principle in *Morgan*, allowing a defence of unreasonable mistake in self-defence, represents an unnecessary and undesirable movement towards a more subjectivist position. However, an objectivist element was still retained, following the decisions in *Beckford* and *Williams (Gladstone)*, in that the force used had to be reasonable in the circumstances as the defendant believed them to be. It was the defendant's mistaken perception of the circumstances which did not have to be reasonable, not the degree of force used in those perceived circumstances.

Unfortunately, perhaps, even this last remaining vestige of objectivism appears to have been purged from the law of mistaken self-defence as a result of the decision of the Court of Appeal in *R v Scarlett* (1993). The defendant, a landlord of a public house, had bundled out a drunken trespasser who fell down a flight of five steps into the street where he struck his head causing an injury from which he died. The trial judge directed the jury that if the defendant had used excessive force and this had been the cause of death, the defendant was guilty of constructive manslaughter. He was convicted and appealed. Beldam LJ, quashing the conviction, restated the *Williams (Gladstone)* rule, but then added:

... and provided he believed the circumstances called for the degree of force used, he was not to be convicted even if his belief was unreasonable.

This seems to suggest that the accused is not only entitled to be judged on the basis of his own mistaken belief as to what the circumstances were, but also that he is entitled to be judged according to his own assessment of how much force was necessary in those circumstances. The direction to the jury would now appear to be that they should not convict unless satisfied that the defendant was using more force than *he* believed necessary in the circumstances as *he* believed them to be. If this is correct, the notion of any objective element in the law of mistaken self-defence has been completely abandoned with each defendant becoming the arbiter of what degree of force is called for.

Consent

R v Brown and Others (1992)

The appellants in the above case were a group of sado-masochistic homosexuals who had, over a 10-year period, willingly participated in the commission of various acts of violence against each other. These acts, which included whipping, cutting and branding, took place in private and in each case the passive partner or victim consented to what was done and suffered no permanent injury. At first instance, following a ruling by the trial judge that the consent of the victim afforded no defence, the men pleaded guilty to offences under s 47 and s 20 of the Offences Against the Person Act 1861 and appealed, ultimately to the House of Lords.

The question before their Lordships was whether the prosecution has to prove lack of consent where A wounds or assaults B occasioning him actual bodily harm in the course of a sado-masochistic encounter before they can establish A's guilt under s 20 or s 47 of the Offences Against the Person Act 1861. By a majority decision of three to two (Lords Mustill and Slynn dissenting) the House dismissed the appeals and confirmed the convictions. It is difficult to identify any legal reasoning for distinguishing between cases where consent would negate liability and those, like the present one, where it would not. On the contrary, their Lordships appeared content to allow this issue to be resolved on a case by case basis by reference to policy considerations. In relation to the specific facts in question Lord Lowry stated that:

... it is not in the public interest that people should try to cause, or should cause, each other actual bodily harm for no good reason and (...) Sado-masochistic homosexual activity cannot be regarded as conducive to the enhancement or enjoyment of family life or conducive to the welfare of society.

Criticisms of the decision in *Brown*

One unfortunate effect of the decision in *Brown* is that a defendant who commits an ordinary assault or battery with consent, and without any intention to cause bodily harm, will not be criminally liable if no bodily harm is caused, but will be guilty of an offence under s 47 if bodily harm happens to result. This strange and manifestly unjust position has arisen because their Lordships approved the earlier decision in *AG's Reference No 6 of 1980* (1981) which held that the defence of consent was available in relation to common assault, but is not available, other than in a few exceptional situations, in relation to the s 47 offence. The position is compounded by the decision in *R v Savage* (1991), which established that the *mens rea* for the s 47 offence must relate to the initial assault, but need not extend to the resulting actual bodily harm.

However, most of the criticism which has been made of *Brown* relates to the paternalistic and anti-libertarian policy informing the decision. From this perspective the decision is seen as a fundamental invasion of privacy, a denial of the diversity of sexual expression and an attempt to limit the scope of individual sexual freedom (eg L Bibbings and P Alldridge 'Sexual Expression, Body Alteration, and the Defence of Consent' (1993) *Journal of Law and Society* p 356).

Another criticism is that the fundamental issue of whether there should be complete freedom to act consensually or liability for all harms, or some compromise position seems to have been inadequately resolved. Clearly, in line with existing authorities, the House of Lords has adopted a compromise solution, but it has failed to indicate the precise nature of that compromise by establishing a rule for distinguishing between cases where a defence of consent will succeed and those where it will not. Instead, it prefers to rely on complicated and detailed considerations of policy arguments in each individual case, while at the same time denying its policy-making role. As Marianne Giles concludes ('*R v Brown*: Consensual Harm and the Public Interest' (1994) *Modern Law Review* p 101):

This is judicial law-making at its worst and most confused – unchallengeable because unacknowledged. Paternalism triumphs, and it is the paternalism of an unelected, unrepresentative group who use but fail to openly acknowledge that power.'

European developments

Some of the defendants in *Brown* have expressed an intention of taking the case to the European Court of Human Rights on the ground that the decision contravenes Article 8 of the European Convention on Human Rights which guarantees respect for private and family life. This article only permits interference with the right of respect for private life in so far as it is:

... necessary in a democratic society in the interests of national security, public safety or the economic well-being of the country, for the prevention of disorder or crime, for the protection of health or morals.

If the case does indeed come before the European Court of Human Rights it will be decided upon the basis of whether the national authority acted within the scope allowed them by Article 8 and whether that action was in proportion to the social need claimed for it.

Revision Notes

Insanity

Where the defendant claims to have been suffering at the time of the offence from some sort of mental disturbance or impairment, then automatism, insanity and, in murder cases, diminished responsibility may all be considered. Automatism, a condition which consists of the body operating without the control of the mind, has been discussed in Chapter 1 and diminished responsibility in Chapter 4.

Although insanity may also be an issue where the defendant has been remanded in custody, or at the beginning of the trial itself, most undergraduate courses concentrate on insanity in relation to the defendant's mental state at the time of committing the offence. It is insanity as a defence at the trial which is discussed here.

Definition

In 1843 Daniel M'Naghten, intending to murder Sir Robert Peel, killed his secretary by mistake. Following his acquittal on grounds of insanity the judges formulated the so called *M'Naghten* rules which have since become accepted as providing a comprehensive definition of insanity (*R v Sullivan* (1984)).

According to these rules it must be proved (by the defence, on a balance of probabilities) that at the time the offence was committed the defendant was labouring under such a defect of reason, arising from a disease of the mind, so as not to know the nature and quality of the act he was doing, or, if he did know it, that he did not know that what he was doing was wrong.

The nature and quality of the act
As we have noted, one of the two grounds for establishing insanity under the *M'Naghten* rules is that the defendant's disease of the mind prevented him from being aware of his actions. For example, in *R v Kemp* (1957), the defendant was found not guilty by reason of insanity when he was unaware of his actions during a 'blackout' caused by a disease of the body which affected the mind.

Did not know that the action was wrong
The second ground for establishing the defence is that, because of a disease of the mind, the defendant did not know that his actions were

wrong. 'Wrong' in this context has been interpreted to mean *legally* as opposed to morally wrong (*R v Windle* (1952)).

Disease of the mind

Although medical evidence will be of relevance, whether a particular condition amounts to a disease of the mind is a legal not a medical question.

It seems that any disease which affects the functioning of the mind is a disease of the mind. Examples would include epilepsy, diabetes, arteriosclerosis and even sleepwalking (*R v Hennessy* (1989); *R v Kemp* (1957); *R v Burgess* (1991)).

In the Canadian case of *Rabey* (1977), it was held that a 'disassociative state' resulting from '... the ordinary stresses and disappointments of life which are the common lot of mankind ...' did not amount to an external cause. It follows that evidence of such a 'disassociative state' would indicate a disease of the mind. However, evidence of a disassociative state resulting from something qualitatively different to the *ordinary* stresses of life, for example a rape attack, would indicate an external cause (*R v T* (1990)).

A malfunctioning of the mind is not a disease of the mind if it is caused by some external factor such as a blow to the head or the consumption of alcohol or drugs (*R v Quick* (1973); *R v Sullivan* (1984)). Such an external cause might form the basis of a plea of non-insane automatism, providing it resulted in a total loss of control of the mind over the body (see Chapter 1).

Infancy

Rationale

The doctrine of *mens rea* is based on the presumption that criminal liability should only be imposed on those who are capable of understanding the nature and foreseeing the consequences of their actions. Since it is generally assumed that children below a certain age lack this capacity, it follows that they should not be held responsible for acts which if committed by an adult would be criminal.

Children under 10 years of age

There is an *irrebuttable* presumption that a child under the age of 10 at the time of the alleged offence lacks the capacity to form the requisite *mens rea* (s 50 Children and Young Persons Act 1933).

Children between the ages of 10 and 14 years of age

Traditionally, there was a presumption, where a child was between the ages of 10 and 14 at the time of the offence, that he or she was not capable of forming the *mens rea* for the crime in question. This presumption could be rebutted if the prosecution could prove not only the *actus reus* and *mens rea*, but also that the child acted with *mischievous discretion*. It would seem that 'mischievous discretion' means that the child knew that what he or she was doing was seriously wrong (*R v Gorrie* (1919)).

However, the Divisional Court has recently decided that this rebuttable presumption that a minor between the ages of 10 and 14 was incapable of committing a crime no longer existed in English law (*C (A Minor) v DPP* (1994)).

Children over 14 years of age

Children over 14 incur criminal liability on proof of *actus reus* and *mens rea* in the same way as adults.

Intoxication

The courts have distinguished between voluntary and involuntary intoxication.

Voluntary intoxication

Self-induced intoxication is not so much a defence, but rather a denial of *mens rea* based upon mistake. Evidence of drunkenness is introduced to make the mistake more credible.

Alcohol and 'dangerous drugs'

Intoxication, negating *mens rea*, resulting from the voluntary consumption of alcohol or drugs generally recognised to be 'dangerous' will constitute a defence to crimes of *specific* intent, but not to those of *basic* intent (*DPP v Majewski* (1984)).

Intoxication other than by alcohol or 'dangerous' drugs

Intoxication, negating *mens rea*, resulting from the voluntary consumption of 'non-dangerous' drugs will constitute a defence not only in relation to crimes of specific intent, but also in relation to those of basic intent, provided the defendant has not been reckless in consuming them (*R v Bailey* (1983); *R v Hardie* (1984)).

The specific/basic intent distinction

Unfortunately, there is no clear overarching principle for distinguishing between crimes of specific and basic intent. However, it is suggested, as a pragmatic guide, that crimes which can be committed recklessly will be those of basic intent and those requiring evidence of intent, specific intent (*MPC v Caldwell* (1982)).

Involuntary intoxication

Involuntary intoxication which negates *mens rea* will be a defence to crimes of both basic and specific intent. Indeed, following *R v Kingston* (1993), it now seems that the defence will be available even if the defendant formed an intention to commit the offence, provided there is evidence that he would not have done so, but for the drink.

However, if the defendant knows that he is drinking alcohol, but is mistaken as to its strength, the rules relating to voluntary intoxication apply (*R v Allen* (1988)).

Mistake

Mistake of fact

A mistake of fact is a defence where it prevents the defendant from forming the *mens rea* for the crime in question. For example, if the defendant mistakenly, but honestly, believes that the woman he is having intercourse with consents, he will not be guilty of rape.

The mistake must be an honest one, but it need not be a reasonable one (*DPP v Morgan* (1976)).

Where the offence in question can be committed negligently, then, in order to negate *mens rea*, the mistake must be not only honest, but also reasonable (*R v Tolson* (1889)).

Where strict liability is imposed even a reasonable mistake will not excuse.

A mistake of fact made while the defendant was intoxicated should be ignored. Thus, in *R v O'Grady* (1987) a defence of self-defence failed where the intoxicated defendant mistakenly believed he needed to defend himself.

Necessity

Rationale

The essence of the defence is that the defendant committed the crime in question in order to avoid an even greater evil. There are two reasons for recognising a defence of necessity in these circumstances:

- it is unjust to punish a defendant for doing something that a reasonable person would have done in the same circumstances; and
- the law should encourage a defendant to choose the lesser and avoid the greater evil on grounds of public policy.

Availability

Despite the above rationale the courts have traditionally been somewhat reluctant to recognise a full blown defence of necessity. Indeed, in *R v Dudley and Stephens* (1884), Lord Coleridge CJ referred approvingly to Hale's assertion (1 Hale PC 54) that necessity would not be available as a defence to theft of food and then went on to doubt whether it could ever be raised as a defence to homicide. This argument, at least in relation to homicide, has more recently received the support of the House of Lords in *R v Howe* (1987).

Although clearly there never has been a wholesale recognition of the defence of necessity, it has, nevertheless, been accepted on a piecemeal basis, in relation to both statute and common law.

The statutory defence

The following statutory provisions contain what amounts to the defence of necessity, although it is not often explicitly referred to in this way:

- s 5(2)(b) Criminal Damage Act 1971;
- s 1(1) Infant Life (Preservation) Act 1929;
- s 1(4) Abortion Act 1967.

Necessity at common law

During the 1980s, in cases such as *R v Willer* (1986), *R v Conway* (1989) and *R v Martin* (1989), the courts have shown a greater willingness to recognise the defence of necessity, at least in relation to road traffic offences.

On the basis of *Conway* and *Martin* it would appear that where there is some evidence of necessity the matter should be left to the jury with the following direction:

- had the defendant felt compelled to act by what he perceived to be the grave danger of the situation? If so;
- would a sober person of reasonable firmness sharing the characteristics of the accused have responded to the perceived threat by acting as the accused had?

If the answers to both these questions are in the affirmative, the defence of necessity, always assuming it to be available, will be established.

Duress

Duress and necessity

The defences of duress and necessity are closely related. Indeed, the courts in cases such as *Conway* and *Martin* (above) did not explicitly refer to necessity, but to 'duress of circumstances', a phrase also adopted in the Draft Criminal Code Bill of 1989. Although both defences involve a situation where the defendant is faced by a choice of two evils, the major difference between them is the source of the evil. In necessity, the defendant is forced by *circumstances* to break the law, whereas in duress the source of the evil is the threat of another *person*.

Definition

The defence of duress consists of a plea that the defendant felt compelled to commit a crime because of an immediate threat of death or serious bodily harm by another person.

Availability

Because the courts want to encourage people to resist giving in to the pressures to commit crime they have limited the availability of duress. In particular, the defence is not available in relation to murder or to an accomplice to murder (*R v Howe* (1987), or in relation to attempted murder (*R v Gotts* (1991)). In addition, the defence is not available in relation to some forms of treason.

Also the defence of duress is not available to those who voluntarily join criminal groups and are then forced to commit the type of crime for which the group is renowned (*R v Sharp* (1987)).

However, if the defendant is forced to commit an offence of a type which he could not have been expected to foresee when he joined the criminal organisation he may still be able to rely on the defence (*R v Shepard* (1988)).

Onus of proof

If there are no facts from which the defence might reasonably be inferred in the prosecution's case, then the defendant has to produce some evidence of duress. Once this has been done the onus of disproving duress rests on the prosecution.

The direction for duress

The direction to be given to the jury where the defendant raises the defence of duress, is that laid down by the Court of Appeal in *R v Graham* (1982), as approved by the House of Lords in *R v Howe* (1987).

The jury should consider whether the defendant was compelled to act as he did because, on the basis of the circumstances as he honestly believed them to be, he thought his life was in immediate danger? If so, would a sober person of reasonable firmness sharing the defendant's characteristics have responded in the same way to the threats?

If the answers to both these questions is 'yes' the defence of duress is established. The above direction is very similar to those we have already noted for establishing both necessity and provocation.

Coercion

Coercion is a special version of duress which is only available to a wife who commits an offence (other than treason or murder) in the presence of, and under the coercion of, her husband.

The defence appears to be somewhat broader than duress as it encompasses 'pressure' as well as threats of physical violence (*R v Richman* (1982)).

Self defence and s 3(1) Criminal Law Act 1967

The common law allows the citizen to use reasonable force to protect his own person, his property and the person of another. In addition, s 3(1) of the Criminal Law Act 1967 permits the use of reasonable force in order to prevent crime or to arrest offenders.

Self-defence is similar to necessity and duress in the sense that the defendant will be faced with a choice of evils. The defendant will either commit a crime, perhaps homicide or a serious assault, or submit to harm being inflicted on himself, his property or the person of another.

However, unlike necessity and duress, self-defence or s 3(1), can constitute a complete defence to any crime, including murder and treason.

Reasonable force

Only reasonable force may be used in self-defence, defence of property or another, crime prevention and lawful arrest. However, what is reasonable depends upon the circumstances; force which might be reasonable to prevent a violent attack upon the person could be unreasonable in relation to a less serious crime.

In *R v Williams (Gladstone)* (1984) it was established that the defendant commits no offence if the force used was reasonable in the circumstances *as he believed them to be*. Thus, it appeared that an objective concept of reasonableness was to be applied in the context of a subjective interpretation of the circumstances.

However, the above principle seems to have been modified by the Court of Appeal in *R v Scarlett* (1993). This decision suggests that the defendant is not only entitled to be judged on the basis of his own mistaken belief as to what the circumstances were, but that he is also entitled to be judged according to his own assessment of how much force was necessary in those circumstances. If this is right it would appear that the objective concept of reasonableness has been abandoned in favour of the defendant's own view.

Consent

Scope

Although most textbooks consider consent in relation to assaults it should be remembered that the consent of the owner is a complete defence to theft and criminal damage. Moreover, sexual offences, such as rape, usually require proof not only that the victim was not consenting, but also that the accused knew or was reckless as to this lack of consent.

Availability

On grounds of public policy the courts have restricted the availability of the defence. Consent is not available in relation to:

* murder or manslaughter (even if the victim begs to be killed because he is terminally ill and in intense pain);
* a fight, other than in the course of an organised sport, played according to the rules (*AG's Reference No 6 of 1980* (1981));
* the *deliberate* infliction of *bodily harm* (*R v Brown and Others* (1993)).

However, the courts are prepared to allow the defence in relation to:

* lawful sporting activity according to the rules;
* medical and dental treatment carried out by qualified practitioners;
* rough horseplay, where the victim has consented to the risk of harm (*R v Jones* (1987); *R v Atkin and Others* (1992)).

Consent and mistake

An honest belief (but not necessarily a reasonable belief) that the victim was consenting will negate the *mens rea* of the defendant (*DPP v Morgan* (1976); *R v Kimber* (1983)). Of course, this is provided the offence in question is one where the defence of consent is recognised.

Consent obtained by deception

If the consent of the victim was obtained by deception or fraud it will be a valid defence provided it relates to a *non-fundamental* matter, but will be void where it relates to a *fundamental* matter (*R v Williams* (1923)).

A fundamental mistake occurs where the victim consents to something which is *qualitatively* different to that which he thought he was consenting to. For example, if A consents to have sexual intercourse with B in the mistaken belief that B is a film star, the consent will still be valid. A is not fundamentally mistaken about the nature of the act, there is merely a non-fundamental mistake about the status of B. However, if A believes that what they are going to do is a yoga exercise, she is fundamentally mistaken about the nature of the activity and her consent will be rendered void.

Index